# Curing
# Your Dog's
# Bad Habits

# Curing Your Dog's Bad Habits

*Treating Behavioral Problems*

Danny Wilson

 **Sterling Publishing Co., Inc.  New York**

*Some of the suggestions in this book for the treatment of your dog's problems need careful application, particularly in the case of aggressive dogs. Accurate diagnosis is also necessary if treatment is to be successful. Seek help first if you have any doubts about your dog's problem.*

*The author and the publisher do not accept any responsibility for any loss, damage, injury or inconvenience sustained by any person or any pet as a result of using the methods or treatment outlined in this book.*

Library of Congress Cataloging-in-Publication Data

Wilson, Danny
Curing your dog's bad habits : treating behavioral problems / Danny Wilson.
p. cm.
Includes index.
ISBN 0-8069-0514-X
1. Dogs—Behavior. 2. Dogs—Psychology.
3. Animal behavior therapy. I. Title.

SF433.W54 1993
636.7'0887—dc20                    93-25421
                                   CIP

Published 1993 by Sterling Publishing Company, Inc.
387 Park Avenue South, New York, N.Y. 10016
Originally published in Australia by Lansdowne Publishing Pty Ltd
© 1993 Lansdowne Publishing Pty Ltd
Distributed in Canada by Sterling Publishing
c/o Canadian Manda Group, P.O. Box 920, Station U
Toronto, Ontario, Canada M8Z 5P9
Printed and bound in Singapore
by Kyodo Printing Co (S'pore) Pte Ltd
All rights reserved.

Sterling ISBN 0-8069-0514-X

*This book is dedicated to a great man who accepted me as his son and who over the years has had enormous faith in me, "the greatest Dad in the world", Eddie Richards.*

# Acknowledgments

I sincerely thank the following people who have helped and supported me throughout my life, and are all part of this book:

Rod Bray, veterinarian, for nurturing my love of animals and teaching me so much during the early years.

My wife Sylvia, who shares my love of animals, for her love and her unwavering belief in me.

My son Anthony, for his patience over the years when I could not always be there.

My Mum Rose, my sisters Rosanna, Marie (Betty) and Lesley, whom I left behind in England to follow my dream.

Alex Satterthwaite, who was there for me in my early years, and Lilly Richards, who welcomed me with open arms when I arrived in Australia.

Donna Ryan and her magnificent dog, Ceasar.

To all of these people, my sincere thanks.

# About the Author

Renowned dog control and behavioral therapist Danny Wilson was born in north-east England. Danny migrated to Australia in 1981.

Danny has produced several videos to help save the employees of local councils and government utilities from being harassed or bitten by strange dogs. His techniques have had excellent results, and this stems from their simplicity in both concept and execution.

His love of dogs led him into a professional career that has spanned more than a quarter of a century. He has delivered many lectures and trained dogs for movies, plays, farm work and domestic situations where he works with dogs in their own environment

# CONTENTS

# INTRODUCTION

It is my belief that dogs prefer to be trained. Training makes their lives better balanced and more purposeful and they are accepted by society, which appreciates an obedient hound. An unruly dog is only a reflection of its owner's inability to communicate with it.

As a young boy living in the cold north-east English countryside, my family owned two purebred Whippets, who we named Bones and Spock after the "Star Trek" characters.

Managing dogs as a profession began to interest me when I noticed that a friend's German Shepherd would bite him, yet never bite me. I began to realize that this dog had greater respect for me than for its owner, even though I spent less time with it. I also began to wonder why some dogs act erratically toward their owners, while others show great respect for and good manners toward the dog's best friend, the human. I began observing dog behavior very closely and worked with the dog experts in our village.

From this small beginning, I went on to work with thousands and thousands of dogs in both hemispheres, progressing from the wide-eyed student with an interest to a specialist in determining and solving the behavioral problems of dogs. My home therapy is usually divided equally between dog and owner. Most problems stem from a lack of understanding on the owner's part. Once the owner understands why the dog becomes neurotic, I can help solve most of its behavioral problems.

Most behavioral problems in dogs start at an early age, although they may not become apparent until the dog is an adolescent (seven to 14 months of age). Its behavior may be not unlike that of the wayward teenager. This is the most crucial stage in the relationship between dog and owner. Many an owner gives up on a dog at this age because of its behavioral disorders, so a good grounding at an early age is imperative.

By following my instructions closely, you should be able to select and rear a puppy responsibly, identify your dog's temperament type, correct its current behavioral disorders, and prevent all manner of problems from even occurring. The importance of consistency and patience will be revealed, and you will be given simple and really effective methods that will solve most of those annoyances. You will learn how your reaction to a dog is important and that the complicated way humans communicate with each other can confuse and even destroy relationships with our four-legged friends.

If you follow these methods most young dogs can be cured within hours and, given time, even old dogs will learn new tricks. Where a dog proves particularly difficult, however, be cautious for the sake of both its safety and yours, and call in an expert if necessary.

I hope that the techniques in this book, in showing how to communicate on a dog's level, will help create a greater understanding between humans and dogs. I do not believe there are bad dogs—only misunderstood dogs.

## Chapter One

# Why Does Your Dog Misbehave?

*We know dogs can misbehave in so many ways, causing havoc. We have all seen dogs chasing cars, attacking the mailman, biting children, jumping fences, causing car accidents, or chasing and killing animals. But why do they do this?*

*Dogs will do only what their instincts tell them, unless they are trained to do otherwise. They do not have a conscience or knowledge of what is right or wrong. Because of this, they can act in ways we see as misbehavior. Just how much of a problem this behavior may cause depends on how strictly the owner controls the dog.*

# The dog in society

To understand the importance of control by the owner, we have to understand the nature of the dog. The domesticated dog is a member of our society, but it is still largely governed by its natural instincts, and has many of the same behavior patterns as its wild ancestors.

Over a significant period of time, humans have managed to breed out many of the wilder attributes from dog species. Today's domestic pet is much like a perpetual puppy, dependent in many ways on its owner. Humans chose to breed out qualities like roaming or fear when challenged so that dogs were more likely to stay close to home.

The wild dog was a pack animal. Pack members lived in close co-operation with each other to ensure their survival. The pack leader was the central figure, the most dominant dog in the pack. Young wild dogs would have been dependent on other pack members for food and protection, and would have behaved in a suitably submissive manner, unwilling to threaten the hierarchy and lose its protection. Then, as they matured, like teenagers testing the limits of their autonomy, they would begin to establish their own positions in the hierarchy of the pack. They would also begin testing the pack leader to see if it was still dominant.

The pack leader did not rule throughout its life. As it aged, it started to display signs of inconsistency and lose its touch. When this happened, the other members of the pack challenged it. It was every dominant dog's instinct to become leader of the pack, and the dominance of the leader ensured

# CLANCY'S CAPERS

Clancy was a two-year-old rogue Rottweiler. His owners had no control over him, but despite this they let him out daily into the streets. On one particular day, he lost that freedom. Events went something like this.

A baker's delivery van was parked outside a cake store in the main street of a small suburb. Clancy scented freshly baked cream cakes and climbed into the back of the van to investigate. The driver, returning with empty cake trays, saw with horror the large Rottweiler standing in the van with cream on its face. He screamed with terror at Clancy.

In panic, Clancy jumped from the van, knocking the driver to the ground and sending the trays flying. To witnesses, it appeared that Clancy had attacked the driver. Their shouts made Clancy bolt across the busy road. A car braked and swerved, crashing into the baker's van. A storekeeper rang the police to inform them of a savage dog on the rampage.

Meanwhile Clancy arrived home, hardly any worse for his experience, and still sporting the cream on his jaws. An hour later the local police officer walked into the backyard with Clancy's owner; Clancy was playing there peacefully. There was no evidence he knew he had done something wrong. He looked altogether harmless. Despite this, the police officer took the dog away. Witnesses had seen it leap at the van driver, and decided that it was savage and destructive, a danger to society.

Clancy was always creating some havoc in the town, but this latest caper had been the last straw. He had caused thousands of dollars' worth of damage. His owners were responsible for the cost, and the dog was only returned to them after they had paid a large fine and the cost of the damage. From then on, his owners never let him out again. If only they had received sound advice about their dog's problems, Clancy's future would be much brighter and his present mess could have been avoided.

the pack's strength. There were always younger and stronger dogs waiting in the wings to challenge for leadership. The leader would start finding it more difficult to maintain its hold on the pack, and would eventually be defeated by a younger, more able dog.

A dog that is domesticated is also part of a pack: a pack of which you, the owner, are the leader. As the leader it is your responsibility to provide guidance but you can give your dog the wrong messages by being inconsistent with it, doing one thing one day and then relenting the next. If you are inconsistent in enforcing control, your dog will assume that you are losing your strength as a leader, and that it has control over you. It will misbehave, and create difficulties in your home and in society.

However, your dog will quite happily conform if you act as if you are the leader. If you discipline your dog, and are fair, firm and consistent, you will establish sound pack leadership. Then you will have won your dog's respect, and can act as its controller and protector. You can also serve as its conscience and prevent behavior that is seen as unacceptable to society. How to win your dog's respect is detailed in Chapter Two.

# Behavioral misconceptions

## "My dog knows he's done something wrong"

I have heard this statement from hundreds of dog owners. We like to believe that our animals think in human terms. This is not the case, however. Dogs do not think the way we think. They have no conscience, and do not feel guilt about something we judge as wrong.

To make our dogs acceptable to our society, they must be controlled, and it is the owner who has to enforce that control. Dogs cannot make their own judgments, nor should their behavior remain unchallenged. Rules and regulations about dogs are there not only to protect the general public, but also to protect the dogs themselves.

In Clancy's story, you read how a dog with too much freedom can become a problem, because it has no concept of right or wrong. Clancy's owners lacked control over their dog and did not find proper help for its problems. The unfortunate result was that Clancy became an outcast, a situation this book can help you prevent, or if that is too late, to remedy.

## SHANDY'S SHAKE-UP

Shandy was a 12-month-old Golden Retriever. He was continually pulling washing off the line and trampling it into the muddy ground. He was slapped by his owners each time they discovered the mess. Yet, no matter how many times he was slapped, Shandy continued with his undesirable behavior.

Hitting a dog after the fact only makes it frightened of its owners, and both confused and neurotic. There was no way that Shandy could associate the punishment with any crime as he could not know that the washing was out of bounds and this unexplained aggression from his owners certainly was not getting the message across. If he had known he was doing the wrong thing all along, he would have tried to hide the washing, rather than leaving it there in plain view and getting a belting as well.

The owners had to get the washing itself to reprimand him. My instructions were to select some old clothes, soak some foam rubber in citronella or hot curry powder, and sew the foam rubber into the hems of the clothes. Then these should be hung on the line on their own.

Now each time Shandy bit the clothes he experienced something unpleasant instead of the fun he had previously had. This encouraged him to seek other games instead. Also, he was now being scolded at the time he was doing the wrong thing, not hours later when his owners arrived home and he had totally forgotten what he had done. Shandy was now happy to see his owners, and no longer associated them with beltings, especially when he had no idea what they were for.

A couple of weeks later, I heard that the old clothes had done their job. Shandy now leaves the washing alone. His owners have set up a plaything for him that dangles from the line with his toys in it. This is the only thing he attacks—with his owners' full permission.

## "My dog understands every word I say"

Our language is very complicated for a dog. Dogs do not have the ability to understand us in the same way we understand other human beings. At best they can be taught to understand a few different words and phrases in our language.

Of course, we do like to talk to our animals in the same way we speak to each other. So it stands to reason that we might think that our dogs are little people and understand our every thought. However, by acting this way we only confuse and alienate them. Carrying on a conversation with a dog is really of no benefit to it. It will only look at the speaker in bewilderment, turning its head from side to side in an effort to understand.

Dogs relate to key words, words that are repeated over and over again until they are familiar. They will understand only one or two words for each behavior pattern we want to instill, and they will only understand the words if they are used while the action is actually happening. We cannot sit them down and tell them what they have done wrong. The case history of Shandy clearly illustrates this. It shows that reprimanding your dog

after the fact has no effect at all. Like Shandy, no dog will know it is doing wrong unless the reprimand or bad experience happens at the exact moment it is actually doing the wrong thing. Only then it can relate the words and actions its owner uses to what is happening and make some sense of it.

## A dog is a human's best friend

We often hear this saying, but I believe it should be the other way around: a human is a dog's best friend. I often wonder how the dog would have fared if it had not gotten together with the human. It would probably still be wild, and no doubt considered a threat to society and to domestic stock. It probably would have been hunted like many wild animals, such as the fox or the wolf or the Australian dingo.

I have found in general that the dog is very well catered for. The pet industry is one of the biggest growth industries. Pet products outsell every other product on the

*Never use a news-paper. Try a chain, an atomizer or a stone-filled can.*

*What we call the reprimand chain is just a 3 ft (1 m) length of heavy, round-edged link chain. Like the stone-filled can, it is intended to be a distraction. Throw the chain or the can near your dog's back legs.*

*An atomizer also works well as a reprimand tool if used on a dog that hates water. Say the BAD word sternly as you spray your dog's face. Remember, in all cases of reprimand, praise your dog the moment it behaves.*

*Jumping up can become a major concern not only to yourself but to children and guests as well.*

*Break the habit with a firm "Bad" and a squirt from the atomizer as soon as your dog's front feet leave the ground. If the atomizer does not work for your dog, use the reprimand chain thrown near its hind legs.*

*Pat your dog lavishly the second it hops down and, in future, refrain from patting the dog unless it has all four feet on the ground.*

## CANDY'S CURE

Candy was a 15-month-old Bichon Frise who had everything a dog could possibly want—or so it seemed. Her owner had indulged her dog with every new product on the market. Candy had a water bed, a stereo, seven coats—one for each day of the week—and seven leads to match those coats. She was on a specially controlled diet, and had her own table and chair to sit on while she ate. Nothing was too good for Candy.

Despite all this, Candy was not a happy dog. She had taken to snapping at her owner without any provocation. One night, when the owner got up from her seat at the television set, Candy lunged at her without warning, biting her so severely on the thigh that she had to have hospital treatment and a tetanus injection. Then, in the months that followed, Candy bit and attacked her owner several times, again for no reason.

When I was called in I saw the many visible signs of the owner's love for Candy. She had given her dog all these things to make its life more comfortable. She was at a loss to understand why her dog had chosen to repay her in this way, particularly as she never scolded or hit it.

I could see Candy was totally spoilt, void of any discipline. She was also very unhappy, because she had no direction. The owner mistakenly believed that if she gave her dog everything, the dog would love her in return. But a dog's love is based on respect, and it will not respect someone it can control.

I prescribed therapy for Candy and told her owner that it must be followed on a daily basis. Candy should still have the special things she enjoyed, as these were not making her unhappy. She should also be taught to respect her owner. This method, called conditioning, is described in the next chapter.

Once Candy's owner won her respect, Candy stopped snapping. Having to obey and follow the owner's rules had given her an outlet for her frustrations.

market. We are spending millions of dollars on our beloved canine companions. Nothing is too good for them. They have space-age kennels, toothbrushes, cashmere coats, and the latest in doggy beds and gourmet dog foods.

But as the case study of Candy demonstrates so clearly, dogs need more than these things. In fact, spoiling your dog can be the root of its problems. Provide it with love, discipline and leadership and you'll surely be your dog's best friend.

## Chapter Two

# First Steps to a Well-Behaved Dog

*We have already learnt how a dog relates to our language. Now we look at how a dog learns, and at methods of disciplining our dogs that will take advantage of their way of learning.*

# How a dog learns

There are basically two main components in dog behavior: ancestry and experience. The first covers that instinctive behavior that is very like that of the wild, pack animals to which your dog is related. Your dog has inherited its temperament and other attributes from the dogs from which it has been bred.

Experience, however, is the key to the kind of pet your dog becomes. A dog has a very good memory. Because of this I can teach a dog to heel properly, sit stay, and generally behave well in as little as five to ten minutes! Providing you keep it simple and address the dog in single words, not with complex sentences, your dog can learn quickly and easily. This same memory ability, however, means that a dog can often recall traumas and these may be the real reason behind its apparent misbehavior.

Play is a very important part of a dog's life, and especially so for an adolescent. A young dog should not be deprived of its puppyhood by too

## BOSLEY'S BOSSINESS

We would all agree that particular programs on television can be exceptionally irritating, others that we come to watch with passionate addiction ... but rarely do family members agree on what makes enjoyable viewing. That battle of wills becomes even more difficult when a snarling dog holds the strongest opinion in the house.

When Bosley, a Maltese Terrier, first joined his owners, they thought it was incredibly cute to draw their dog's attention to other dogs on television. Eventually, Bosley had seen enough episodes of *Lassie* and *Rin Tin Tin* to learn when they were broadcast and he would sit on the lounge waiting for the shows to begin. Cute too, except if any member of the family changed the channel Bosley would physically attack them. Sick of the biting, Bosley's owners asked me for advice and I suggested they reprimand their dog with a squirt from an atomizer when it attacked. They were allowing their dog to be boss of the house and Bosley had no respect for them. The family called me again about a week later. They couldn't bring themselves to discipline Bosley but they had found a solution that they felt suited them ... they had bought Bosley a television of his own! Oh well, you can't win them all.

Thankfully there was another dog and another family who reached a far easier compromise to their disagreement in taste.

Pud, a two-year-old British Bull Dog, was another dog with strong opinions on television watching. This dog, however, had a vehement hatred for one particular television program. Whenever it came on, she would physically attack the television. I was called in by the owners to stop this furious display. We pre-recorded the program on video and when Pud reacted fiercely to the replay, I threw down a can filled with ball bearings and yelled "Bad". She stopped her attack, I praised her and, with a bit of repetition, she was cured. Now when a program comes on that she doesn't like, she simply leaves the room. A better solution than the one Bosley's owners chose.

much training. Short training sessions (no longer than ten minutes) are all that is required.

Even play is not all fun, however. It is the way in which dogs in the wild learn to fight and survive and the way you, unconsciously, may be teaching your dog inappropriate behavior. Allowing your pup to bite your hand while playing, for example, means it will be difficult for that dog to understand why it is not allowed to really bite at other times. Chasing a dog may encourage it to run away rather than come when it is called.

You must always be aware of the consequences of any behavior you encourage or, like the owners of Bosley in our case study, you may find that what was cute and playful behavior at first develops into a real problem.

# Restraints

Understanding how your dog learns will help you teach it how to behave. Several restraining devices can be used to help discipline your dog. I will refer to them throughout this book as a major part of the treatment for behavioral problems.

Let's take a look at the tools:

All dogs need leads, both for walks outside your backyard and as a training device. Buy a strong webbed lead, as the fabric has some "give" and will not break easily.

If your dog gives you problems while walking, you may also need a check chain, or check collar. This is a thick-gauge chain about 4 inches (10 cm) longer than the dog's neck width. (Turn to "Walking Problems" in Chapter Four for more about using this.)

You will need a reprimand chain with which to stop your dog in its tracks when it does something it should not be doing. This should be a length of heavy, high-tensile, steel link chain, about 3 ft (1 m) long, with rounded edges so that if it accidentally makes contact with the dog it will not hurt it. See our section on "Conditioning and Reprimanding" later in this chapter for advice on using this chain.

You can also reprimand your dog using a can filled with stones, or an atomizer filled with water. Both of these have the effect of startling the dog and stopping it in its tracks while it is doing something it should not be doing. You will be shown in this book when it is appropriate to use these restraining devices.

Food can provide a welcome incentive when teaching a dog, and doggy treats are often mentioned in this book as a training tool, but be careful of using food as a bribe. Bribery is often attempted with a thieving dog where food or another item that is not needed is swapped for the item the dog has in its possession. But this merely creates a compromise, not a cure. It will only ensure that unacceptable behavior continues and perhaps worsens. Like a child screaming for chocolate in the supermarket because it knows it will eventually get what it wants, a dog that is bribed will keep doing the wrong thing because it knows this will produce rewards and the dog feels it has control.

# Conditioning and reprimanding your dog

The key to having a dog without behavioral problems is gaining its respect. The process of gaining its respect is what I call conditioning. It involves training your dog to respond to a certain reprimand. Your dog should always be conditioned first before you treat it for a problem. Then you know it will be ready to accept the treatment.

Also remember that your dog is not deliberately being naughty when it misbehaves. As you read in the preceeding chapter, it is only following its natural instincts by testing your control. It is important that you do not get angry with the dog while training it. Remember that if you are firm and patient toward your dog it will respect you, and once it respects you it will see you as its leader and will no longer misbehave.

Do not be deterred by the concept of discipline. It does not mean lack of care and love, in fact it indicates the opposite.

To condition your dog, you will be using the same method repeatedly, and rewarding the dog when it does what it is supposed to.

Start by placing your dog in a sit position on a check chain and lead. Your first objective is to familiarize it with a reprimand. The single word I like to use is "Bad", uttered in a deep, guttural tone, like a dog's growl. The instant your dog moves from the sit position, use the BAD word. Remember, this is the only sound the dog should hear when it is being reprimanded. Say "Good dog" in a soft tone when the dog stays in position. Just be persistent. Finally, your dog will be effectively conditioned to stop whatever it is doing wrong when it hears the BAD word.

To reprimand, it is simply a matter of growling "Bad" at the dog at the exact moment it does whatever you want it to stop doing. When the dog does stop, follow quickly with a pat and praise.

Now you are ready to control your dog's behavior problem using a reprimand chain. First set up a situation where the dog will do something it should not be doing, such as chasing a stranger. Using the BAD word, throw the chain at the ground near the dog's hind legs. As soon as the misbehavior stops, pat the dog and praise it lavishly. Keep going with a cycle of reprimand and praise until the dog stops misbehaving.

It is important to try to remember at all times how your dog may perceive your actions or you could end up re-inforcing negative behavior like Bear's owner did in our case study.

# Why the BAD word?

My own theory on reprimanding is based on the way one dog would reprimand another. Let us look at this process. A dog does not really want to fight another dog in the pack unless it is forced to. A growl is usually sufficient—in terms of body language it is easy to interpret. The growling dog will stand very tall and rigid, not making any quick moves. A dog flat on its back or crouched down would find it hard to control a tricky situation with another dog.

We know that a dog will respond to a growl. We therefore use a short, harshly uttered word such as "Bad" that the dog would not otherwise hear in normal speech.

We have also seen that body language is important when a dog is delivering a reprimand or receiving one. I have found that if the owner is either sitting or lying down while delivering a command, most dogs will disobey even if the command is familiar to them, one to which they generally respond. When we lose height, as far as the dog is concerned we lose authority.

We can condition our dogs to obey at these times. During training, while the dog is in a stay position, that is, either sitting or lying with its front legs stretched out on the ground, we can crouch or sit down. This will accustom the dog to obeying us no matter what position we are in.

## BEAR'S BELLIGERENCE

I was called in to help with an 18-month-old Belgian Shepherd called Bear who had suffered a frightening experience as a young pup. When Bear was four months old, a man entered Bear's yard to scare out some other dogs that had strayed in. The man acted with great aggression, kicking and chasing the dogs as Bear watched terrified. From that time, Bear feared that he would receive the same kind of treatment from all strangers and would attempt to attack any that entered his territory. When I arrived at Bear's house I was met by an onslaught of barking and growling, with Bear's owner trying her best to quieten him by yelling "Bear" each time he leapt at the door. When I asked her to open the door, she was horrified. Bear charged at me but stopped short, barking madly as I stood my ground. He jumped back and forward noisily and I noticed that each time he backed up near his owner she would attempt to console him by patting him and speaking reassuringly. The problem was that the dog was interpreting this as support for his antics and thought he was being praised for his aggression. Meanwhile, I reached into my bag and pulled out my reprimand chain. Handing it to Bear's owner, I instructed her to throw it at the dog's feet when he next lunged at me, and yell "Bad". After only two attempts, Bear ran outside after which his owner told him softly that he was a good boy. Bear ran to her for a pat and then sat in front of me and offered me his paw.

Until we have reached this stage with our dogs, we must be conscious of our body language when reprimanding. We should not make any quick crouching movements, push with our hands or point.

The BAD word should be delivered with a growling sound. We should never reprimand a dog using its name in a reprimand tone. The dog's name should only be used to attract its attention.

Timing is also very important when reprimanding. The growled "Bad" must be delivered at the precise moment the dog does the wrong thing, not seconds later. The reprimand must stop as soon as the dog stops misbehaving and praise should begin at exactly that time. In this way, you do not allow for any confusion or misinterpretation by your dog. If you get the timing right and are disciplined and constant in your approach, success is ensured. You will see the negative effects of mistimed reprimands in the case study about Harry's havoc.

## HARRY'S HAVOC

Harry, a 15-month-old Cocker Spaniel, was refusing to stay in the laundry at night, where he was supposed to sleep. He would scratch and bark at the door, disturbing his owner.

The owner told me she would reprimand Harry when he did this, by hitting him with a rolled newspaper and yelling at him. But nothing she did seemed to work.

"Have you caught him in the act of barking and scratching?" I asked.

"Oh yes, we have, many times. When he is barking and scratching, I jump out of bed, grab the paper and sneak to the door, open the door and smack him."

I pointed out to her that this was not exactly catching Harry in the act. The door that he had been scratching and barking at was now open, and he was no longer misbehaving. Instead, he was looking at his owner!

The most effective way to solve that particular problem was to throw something at the door that would make a loud bang, and yell "Bad" at the same time. In this way the dog would be reprimanded while it was barking and scratching, not seconds later when it would not understand the reprimand.

A few loud reprimands later, Harry was quite content to remain in the laundry.

# Scene setting

Catching your dog in the act can be difficult. One way of getting around this problem is to set a scene that will encourage your dog to misbehave while you are present and on the alert—have a stranger to the dog come visit or have a friend walk a dog past your yard, to suit the particular problem. Better still if you can manage to remain hidden but watchful before your dog misbehaves so that it will learn to behave properly even in your absence. Leap out from your hiding space and reprimand your dog as you catch it in the act. After a few repeat performances, it will believe that your disciplining presence is a possibility even when it seems that you are not around.

# STEPS TO A WELL-BEHAVED DOG

1. Remember, dogs do not understand our language. Use single words and keep them simple.

2. Always be aware of the behavior you may be encouraging, even in play.

3. Use a strong webbed lead and check chain or check collar to keep your dog under control.

4. You must gain your dog's respect through conditioning before you can treat its behavioral problems.

5. Distract your dog from bad behavior with a reprimand chain or a stone-filled can thrown next to the dog's hind legs, preferably on a hard surface.

6. An atomizer filled with water may also be used as a reprimand tool.

7. The word "Bad" should be spoken in a loud, growling tone as part of conditioning and reprimanding.

8. A reprimand should be delivered at the exact moment a dog misbehaves.

9. Praise, through patting and kindly spoken words, is essential the moment a dog stops misbehaving.

10. It is necessary for you to maintain your role as "pack leader" over the dog to avoid behavioral problems.

# Chapter Three

# Prevention Is Better Than Cure

You may be faced with a problem dog like those you have read about in Chapter One, or those in the case studies in Chapter Four. But if you are not a dog owner yet and are about to buy a puppy, or if you are about to get another dog, you may find you will never have to deal with any of these problems. The secret lies in selecting your puppy carefully, and disciplining it in the right way from the outset. Condition your dog as outlined in the last chapter, and you will win its respect.

You will also find comments in this chapter on the principles of dog psychology. This should help you to understand how to anticipate and prevent the misbehavior of any dog, young or old.

# Puppy and dog selection

Selecting the right pup is of great importance if you want to have an adult dog that is easy to train and control. A dog that has the wrong temperament can create many headaches for its owner.

A puppy should be no younger than six to 12 weeks of age before being separated from its mother. Any younger is too early, even if the pup has been weaned. Some breeders like to hold on to their puppies for up to three months so that they have a better idea of which pup they will keep for themselves. This is not very fair on the dog as the first weeks of its life are vital for socialization and a pup that is isolated in a kennel and not exposed to many people can suffer paranoia and lasting psychological damage.

Your first step in pup selection should be to choose a well established breeder. The breeder you use is important. A reputable breeder is breeding dogs not only for their physical attributes but also for stable temperaments, and can often help select the right pup to suit your personality. It is likely that an inexperienced breeder would have no idea which pup would be likely to grow into a well-adjusted adult. Most countries have breed registers of purebred dogs, where breeders can register their breeding kennels.

Crossbred dogs can make just as loyal pets as purebred dogs but many people are hesitant to take on a cross-bred pup if they cannot predict the eventual full-grown size. As a basic guideline, a pup is likely to inherit its size from its mother but one should expect the adult dog to be slightly smaller than the larger breed in the cross.

Certain crossbreeds are more desirable than others. Qualities of temperament in a particular breed can be offset by qualities in the crossbreed. For example, a Boxer's bouncy personality may be calmed by the more even character of a Labrador. It is not advisable to choose the offspring of a mix of highly strung breeds or you may end up with a very neurotic dog indeed.

Of course, your new dog may not be a pup but an older pre-loved pet. The benefit of these dogs is that the puppy stage is over and it is easier to see what temperament the dog has developed, particularly how it relates to strange and new environments and people. You will be able to start training the dog immediately but remember that as a newcomer it will require a lot of attention and understanding. Try to discover as much about its background as possible, including details of its diet. It is a good idea to try to bring a beloved item with it from its old home. If you are expecting it to act as a pet-come-guard dog, keep in mind that it will take approximately two weeks before the dog starts to treat its new home as its territory and protect it.

## Behavior patterns to look for

When I am selecting a puppy for someone, I take the pups from the litter one by one to an area away from the others so I can observe their behavior individually. Note that when you lead it away, a well-adjusted pup will follow you freely.

I then take something, such as my wallet, and throw it so that it lands on the ground near the pup (naturally being careful not to hit the pup). A well-adjusted pup will go to investigate the sound straight away. Less stable pups will jump and move away, but will return to investigate fairly quickly; this is still acceptable behavior. The pup that barks at the object, runs away refusing to return to the spot, or crouches down, is of a rather timid nature, and does not have the most desirable temperament for a pet.

I also lift and hold each pup in my arms. A pup that sits still is far more acceptable than the wriggly one. If you are looking for a very submissive type, try rolling the puppy onto its back. If it lies perfectly still it is the one you want.

Be sure, though, that you do know what kind of temperament you prefer in a puppy. Be wary of making a choice that is based on emotion only. In the case study of Crystal, you will read about a soft-hearted couple who took pity on a very timid, frightened pup, and lived to regret it.

It is very, very difficult to train timidness out of a dog and this is one trait that can affect much of a dog's behavior and lead to many other problems.

## CRYSTAL'S CRINGES

Crystal was a black Cocker Spaniel her owners got as a pup from a backyard breeder. When they went to make their choice, all the pups in the litter came out, tails wagging, to greet them — all, that is, except Crystal. The couple asked the breeder about the shy puppy and were told that she might have to be put to sleep. No one seemed interested in taking her because of her shyness. The couple were immediately filled with pity for the timid little creature, and decided to buy her.

Crystal was a difficult pup to handle from the very start. She would cry for hours on end if left alone, and cringe with fear if anyone visited the house. As she grew older, she began growling and barking at visitors, no matter how friendly they were. Her owners became very despondent—entertaining their friends had become a nightmare.

The owners called me in to help with Crystal's antisocial behavior. They mentioned her timid behavior when they went to buy her at the kennels, and questioned whether she might have been mistreated by the breeder. I explained that the breeder would be unlikely to mistreat only one puppy and not the others. Crystal was probably born a timid dog. One of her ancestors, or even her father or mother, had had this type of personality, and she had inherited it, just as humans inherit traits from their parents or ancestors. With a personality disorder like Crystal's, the dog can develop phobias that are very hard to correct. As I advise in this chapter it is possible to identify a timid pup and much better not to select this kind of dog in the first place.

The good news for the owners, though, was that Crystal's behavior could be modified by treatment and follow-up therapy. We could first try the normal types of treatment, such as getting visitors to the house to pat her and tempt her with food. It might work in this case. If it did not, we would have to be very firm indeed to solve her problem.

First I conditioned Crystal, getting her owners to place her on a lead for me. She tried her utmost to bite me, but soon realized I was more dominant, and did as I asked.

After the conditioning was completed I let her off the lead and we arranged for someone to visit the house. As soon as the visitor knocked she sprang up and began showing aggression, barking and growling. We tried treats of food, but she was too upset to eat.

I decided we needed a more forceful approach. I began reprimanding her by throwing the reprimand chain close to her back legs and yelling the BAD word. She flew out of the room, barking as she went. I followed her, repeating the procedure several times. Finally, quite exhausted, she stopped. I patted and praised her, and she climbed onto my lap and licked me. I gave her a cuddle. Then she followed me to the door. I told her owners to let the visitors in. As soon as she caught sight of them she started barking again. I again reprimanded in the same way, and she immediately stopped and ran to me for a pat. All of Crystal's so-called aggression was just bravado; underneath she was a quivering wreck.

With a small amount of follow-up by the owners, Crystal was cured of barking at visitors. She never fully accepted people, and would go and sit in the corner with a worried look on her face when a stranger was about. But for her owners this was a great improvement on the noise they had had to endure.

We cannot change a dog's inherent temperament or personality, but with correct treatment we can modify it to a more acceptable form.

# Choosing a breed to suit your personality

Be sure also to select a breed of dog that will suit your lifestyle and personality, as choosing a dog that is wrong for you could be disastrous. For instance, a frail, docile person would find a dog of a large breed difficult to control, especially if the dog was boisterous or hyperactive. Correspondingly, a timid little dog would not be a suitable match for a person with a strong will.

That is why in this section we take a look at some of the most popular breeds and how their personalities and characteristics fit into the differing requirements of different owners: whether they are people who need dogs with soft, even temperaments or those that are drawn to stronger personalities, those that want the comfort of a "one-person" dog or those, like families with children or with other pets, who would benefit from a dog with a sociable disposition. Some dogs, of course, fall into more than one of these categories.

Potential problems are pinpointed below. Most problems, however, can be avoided by early conditioning and training using the methods outlined in this book. Turn to Chapter Four on "Problems and their Cures" for advice on specific bad habits.

## Softer temperaments

### Beagle
The most amiable of the hound group—a trait which has sometimes worked to its detriment. Being more able to cope than most breeds, they have been used widely in experiments. A soft and cuddly nature makes them great lap dogs. Their most annoying trait is the relentless pursuit of a scent and so need to be trained at a young age to come when called.

### Golden Retriever
Often mistaken for a long-coated Labrador, the Retriever shares many characteristics with that breed but with a softer temperament and less exuberant nature.

### Labrador
One of the world's most popular breeds, their good even temperament has made them great family dogs as well as making them suitable as guide dogs or for use in therapy. Bred mainly as a bird dog to fetch birds for hunters and return them whole and intact, they are very easily trained and can be taught to fetch domestic items like newspapers and slippers. Lovable and energetic, they can, however, be quite destructive in their first two years. Do not be surprised if you find your Labrador sitting near the table begging for food scraps. This breed is prone to obesity unless its diet is watched carefully.

### Old English Sheepdog
Made famous through Walt Disney movies, this breed attracts a lot of attention—be prepared to be stopped in the street by admirers. They make great family dogs due to a soft, amiable temperament and the capacity to romp and play all day long. Their lack of concentration, however, makes training more difficult than usual. Although training should be attempted early, best results are achieved at about two to four years of age.

### Shetland Sheepdog
This is one of the most undemanding breeds known. They are very clean and fastidious dogs although their coat requires much care and

attention. Liking nothing more than to spend hours curled up with their owner, these loving dogs have a very docile temperament that makes them perfect for children and the elderly.

### Siberian Husky

Safe around family, friends and other dogs due to their loving nature, the genetic background of these dogs means that they need to be trained out of pulling from an early age. Howling can also be a difficult behavioral characteristic.

### Whippet

This breed is closely related to the Greyhound and they too love to chase anything that moves. With basic training they are probably better suited to a soft-natured person as they are so easily controlled.

# Dogs that need a firmer hand

### Afghan Hound

It is a pleasure to watch the elegant stride of these dogs as they run (which they love to do) but it can be difficult to get them to stop or to come when called. These dogs require lots of exercise but their energy and loyal, loving natures make them wonderful family pets. It is only exuberance combined with size that requires control.

### Boxer

The strong physique of these dogs is matched by their personality. Very exuberant and bouncy, they are not suited for a soft-natured person as they require a firm hand but they are easy to train. Great for people with lots of energy. They make loyal and loving pets for children as they possess a very amiable nature. Slobbering can be a problem.

### Bull Terrier

Lovable, trustworthy dogs as far as people are concerned but they tend to act unsociably when confronted with other animals. This is understandable as the dogs were bred to control cattle and later as fighting animals. They are quite trainable; their stubbornness is often viewed incorrectly as a lack of intelligence. They are very tough dogs that play hard so they are not suited to a timid person. They are not, however, active dogs and are liable to just drop where they are when they run out of energy, refusing to move. Prone to allergies, they should be kept on a preservative-free diet.

### Cocker Spaniel (English)

Careful breeding over the years has succeeded in eliminating many undesirable traits from this very vivacious breed but they are still prone to swings of temperament if they are not feeling happy with their lot. Quite energetic, these dogs are often like a wound up spring. They need a firm hand as they can be over excitable and erratic if they are not fully controlled. Barking can be a problem if not curbed early.

### Dachshund

Bred to catch rats in their native Germany, this tenacious breed is given to plenty of barking and can cause real problems with their instinctive drive to dig. Despite their diminutive size, they require a very firm hand.

### Dalmation

Possessing an even temperament, Dalmations serve well as guard dogs. This is a very energetic breed that needs room to move and a firm hand to get around their "I'll do it when I'm ready" approach to life.

### Dobermann Pinscher

Bred as guard dogs from Pinschers and Rottweilers, these dogs suffer two main faults: a tendency not to come when called and a habit of chewing through their leads when tied up. Although they are often depicted in the media as ferocious animals, they are actually loving and dependable. Of course, like all dogs, they should be obedience trained from an early age.

### German Shepherd

These are remarkably adaptable dogs, loyal and trustworthy, if trained from an early age. Normally very intelligent, their main faults are usually excessive aggression toward strangers, fence jumping and whole digging. Good guard dogs, German Shepherds are safe provided that you are selective with temperament and avoid timid, frightened types.

### Great Dane

They may be the tallest dogs in the world but they are also among the most docile. Their sheer size does mean that they need to be strictly controlled and trained from an early age and they may be overbearing for small children—though lots of fun.

### Miniature Schnauzer

Cute looks but don't let appearances deceive you. This compact little dog needs a firm hand (as do most German breeds) and lots of exercise, and are not suitable for more easy-going personalities. Wonderful guard dogs that possess a tenacity well beyond their size but barking can be a real problem unless strictly controlled.

### Rottweiler

Known as the "butcher's dog", this breed was used to herd the cattle and protect the day's takings after sale at the markets. It follows that they make great guard dogs. Avoid timid pups and train early to ensure a stable, even temperament. Like Dobermanns, these dogs have suffered from bad (and incorrect) publicity. They are good with children but should be supervised due to their size and a tendency toward over-exuberance. Food aggression can be quite a problem with these dogs.

# "One-person" dogs

### Chihuahua

These are the smallest dogs in the world which makes the breed easy to handle, groom and control, but they can be fairly fussy with food. They originated in Mexico, and their dislike of the cold means they like to snuggle up close to people or under a blanket. "One-person" dogs, they can be rather aggressive to strangers. They also have a tendency toward kleptomania, hiding stolen items in their beds.

### Chow Chow

These fluffy, red dogs with blue tongues were originally bred in China for food! Thank goodness they have instead become popular pets and companions around the world. They make excellent guard dogs who will not be bribed or corrupted. Quite hard to train and definitely a one-person breed, so much so that they are not always suited to the family environment. If you wish to gauge this quality in a potential pet Chow Chow, view the parents of the pup carefully. If the parents are good with children, chances are the pup will be too.

### Maltese

One of the older breeds, these intelligent little dogs are extremely affectionate and are very protective of their houses and owners making them particularly good for people who live alone. Barking can be a problem as regardless of their size they will take on all comers. They can be a little headstrong at times as a result and are one of the breeds that need a firm hand.

### Pekingese

Prone to laziness, these are great lap dogs that are very affectionate and feel at home anywhere—as long as they are close to their owners. They were used as guards in ancient temples and can have a problem with excessive barking if not checked early. In general terms, behavioral problems are relatively minor.

### Shih Tzu

Although not a lot is known about the origins of this breed, it is thought they were used as temple dogs by Tibetan monks. They are good companions but do not take easily to strangers and can be standoffish at times. Quite trainable but do not expect any miracles as Shih Tzus can be stubborn and require patience. Lively dogs yet suitable for small living areas like apartments as they are satisfied with a daily energetic walk.

## Sociable personalities

### Cocker Spaniel (American)

Adorable and loving, American Cocker Spaniels possess a far more stable, even temperament than the English Cocker Spaniel but like that breed they have a problem with excessive barking. They love the company of other dogs and people and are especially good with children.

### Lhasa Apso

Known in Tibet as far back as 900 BC but only introduced into other countries in the 1920s, this is one of the oldest breeds of dogs. They are very loving and respond well to lots of attention but do not like being left alone. Only a low level of exercise is needed which makes them great indoor pets.

### Poodle

A small breed that is excellent with children, a fine family pet and highly intelligent. Their owners must educate them early and provide an outlet for their intellect. They display many tendencies that seem almost human and hate being left alone. Good guard dogs but the breed is renowned for nuisance barking if not checked early. They are also climbing dogs so fences and pens must be very secure.

### Weimaraner

Selectively bred by the German nobility, these all-round hunting dogs possess some fine features. They are proud and aristocratic but also friendly, loyal, protective, alert

*43*

and they excel at obedience training. Very much orientated towards people, they tend to follow their owners everywhere but will occasionally fall victim to wanderlust so good fencing is a must. Some become destructive if left to their own devices for too long.

### West Highland White Terrier

These hardy little dogs are full of mischief but they are not vindictive and are great fun. They love company, especially that of other dogs. Their playfulness makes them winners with children. Their loyalty makes them fine watch dogs. They do have a problem, however, with excessive barking.

# A well-adjusted puppy

In the first few months of a puppy's life you can lay the foundations for a stable, mature adult dog with no behavioral problems. The way a pup is socialized and the degree to which it is socialized will determine how well adjusted it will be as an adult dog.

In line with the well-worn saying that is the title of this chapter,

I am a firm believer in the benefits of preventative training for dogs. Most of the problems I am asked to treat and solve could have been prevented if the owner had had a better understanding of how a dog learns and thinks, and how certain things we do and encourage can cause lasting neurotic behavior.

## Jumping up on people

Dog owners may make the mistake of encouraging a puppy to jump up when it is little because they prefer not to bend down toward it. From then on the dog thinks that this is what it should do if it wants a pat. Even when it is fully grown, the jumping will continue. To cure a
• dog of this habit, first condition it using the methods described in Chapter Two and reprimand the dog with a water atomizer and the BAD word when it jumps up.

## Excessive barking

Young puppies are sometimes encouraged to bark at certain things because this is seen as cute. However, barking from an early age is a danger signal. A well-adjusted pup of good temperament should love everybody, and barking at such an early age displays an undesirable temperament that should definitely be discouraged.

## Jumping over the fence

This habit is usually learned from an early age. The pup's yard may not be secure enough, and it may find it can easily escape. Once it has gained its freedom, it will keep trying to escape even after the yard has been made secure. It is therefore vital to secure your yard from the first day you have your pup.

## Overprotective behavior

An overly aggressive dog has not been socialized properly from an early age. Many times I have seen a dog patted and consoled when it was being aggressive. This aggression may take many forms from protection of food to attacking strangers. Problems of this nature are outlined in Chapter Four. Any form of antisocial behavior should be discouraged. Patting and consoling will be mistaken by the dog as approval of its behavior, and this will then condition it to repeat the performance.

## Early socialization

From the time it is six weeks old a pup should be taken to as many different places as possible, and introduced to people and to other dogs. This is vital for the pup's development and will ensure that it has no fear of strangers of any kind in any circumstance.

The dilemma here is that puppies cannot be fully vaccinated until around about four months of age, and are therefore not safe from disease before that time. I suggest you get around this problem by carrying the unprotected puppy in your arms. This will prevent it from sniffing the ground where diseased dogs may have walked. You can also visit friends who have fenced yards, providing their dogs will not be aggressive to your pup and are immunized. Be aware, though, that some dogs may not necessarily have diseases themselves, but they can be carriers.

## Meeting other animals

A vital step in settling a new dog into a home is its introduction to other animals that live in the household. First ensure that the dog or dogs are disciplined so that you can control any anxious behavior. It is best to place dogs on a check chain and lead for the introductions. Correct any bad behavior, like chasing, barking or aggression, by checking the dog vigorously and using the BAD word to reprimand, praising the dog the moment it stops misbehaving. This is particularly sound when introducing a dog to a cat. The cat is likely to accept the dog quite willingly provided the it is not confronted with a dog that is aggressive or overly exuberant.

If you already own a dog and are thinking of getting another, it is advisable to choose a male to mix with a female. This pair is more likely to cohabit without problems. An older male dog may not readily accept another male entering its territory, regardless of its age. The neutering of male dogs sometimes alleviates this problem but it is not a guaranteed solution. Never leave a young male pup alone with an adult male as a serious attack is possible if the pup oversteps his mark.

There is no easy way to introduce dogs if one or all are behaving anti-socially. A muzzle may help until the dogs become accustomed to each other but like many other situations the key is having control over your dog through respect.

# The time factor

How well adjusted your puppy will be depends entirely on how much time and effort you put in. Puppies have bonding instincts that are very similar to human babies. From birth, a pup forms strong bonds with its mother and litter mates, relying heavily on the security of their family structure. It is just not reasonable to take a puppy away from that family and then just place it in your yard. An animal that is used to being part of a pack then becomes a solitary animal, and will suffer stress and anxiety. Imagine the trauma you could suffer if you were suddenly whisked away to an isolation cell after living in a large city, with a large family. Thankfully, a dog's recovery rate is faster than a human's.

When we take a pup away from its family, the whole bonding process has to start again. The pup will bond to the person who collects it from its litter as this will be the first person it scents other than the litter and its attendant.

Even with an older dog, this bonding occurs rapidly and usually with the person who leads the dog away from its old home. On one occasion I was asked to take a friend's dog to a breeding kennel

for a mating. The process took all day during which time, apart from when she was actually being mated, the dog watched me closely and would not let me out of her sight. She had bonded to me from the moment that I had put on her lead at the start of our journey. If I left the room she would follow me, refusing to go with anyone else.

Because of this bonding process, prospective dog owners should try to be the person to collect the dog, whether a pup or full-grown.

There are a number of things we can do to make the separation less traumatic for a puppy by providing comfort and security. If the pup already has a blanket or basket, try to bring this with the pup. Once home you can help it settle by supplying a hot water bottle (to simulate the warmth of its mother) and a ticking clock (to simulate her heart beat) in a box with a blanket (to give security). A soft, cuddly toy in a shade similar to the pup can lead it to believe it has a litter mate. But most important of all is love and human company.

It is vital to work out just how much time you *can* devote to your pup and how you can fill the void the pup will feel when it is first brought home. If you do not have the time required for a young puppy

# ROCKY'S RECLUSIVENESS

Twelve-month-old Rocky, a German Shepherd, had owners who were very busy professional people. They loved him dearly, but they led hectic lives, and Rocky was forced into a solitary existence. He was lonely every day until his owners returned from work.

By the time I met Rocky he was totally traumatized and had chronic behavior problems: his loneliness had turned him into a recluse, and he became afraid of people and the outside world. He was uncontrollably afraid of everything that moved. His owners could not even take him for a walk.

The therapy I recommended for Rocky involved getting control of him in his own yard first. I calmly and gently won him over, showing him I was not to be feared and he could trust me. He became my best friend within minutes and would not leave my side.

I then started to condition him, as I needed him to be responsive to my commands after conditioning. Bit by bit I took him closer to the gate leading to the street, and eventually took him a little way out. He jumped around at first but I just used the BAD word and he stopped. I patted him the whole time as we walked a short distance, assuring him no harm would come to him while he was by my side. I kept encouraging and patting him until we had walked all the way around the block.

Rocky emerged from his cocoon, realizing the world outside his backyard held exciting things that were not to be feared. His complete cure took two therapy visits from me and about two weeks of follow-up by his owners. He enjoys his life these days, meeting people and other dogs and going for regular walks: now that he is able to be walked without drama, his owners have employed a dog walking service for him. If a dog's owners cannot find time for their dog, there are always alternatives to allowing a dog to suffer alone.

you might be better advised to buy a full grown dog that has already been well adjusted by someone else. Rocky was a classic case of a dog who was maladjusted because of his solitary life as a pup. His story is in our case study.

# Adolescence

Puppies become adolescent dogs when they reach seven months, and are adolescents until they are 14 months old. Research has shown that a majority of people have some kind of problem with their dogs in this "teenage" period. A large number of dogs in this age bracket have been surrendered to animal protection societies.

Our domestic dogs do not behave very differently from their wild ancestors. A young wild puppy would have been very dependent on its mother and the other pack members for protection and food. It would not as a rule have overstepped the mark by trying to assert its authority over other, mature dogs higher up the hierarchy. To do so could have proved fatal, as the young pup would have been no match for an older, much stronger dog. So it would toe the line and

grovel in order to survive. Then, when it was more mature, it could sort out the pecking order and start establishing a place for itself in the hierarchy of the dog world.

Following the same pattern, our young domestic pups will usually obey us and do as we request—that is, until they reach adolescence. Then comes the time for them to spread their wings and test us, their owners, to see where they fit into the social structure. An adolescent dog is not unlike a teenager. Teenagers are trying to sort out their position in life, and many challenge their parents' views and beliefs.

We have to be aware that such a challenge will be mounted by our adolescent dogs, and not be disturbed by it. This knowledge will help us to understand why a dog as it reaches maturity is more difficult to control than the little puppy who was totally dependent on us for protection and guidance.

Our dog's natural instinct is to test us, to assure itself that it is as high up in the pecking order as it can possibly be. In the wild it is vital for the pack's survival that the strongest, most capable and dominant dog leads the pack. The subordinate dogs challenge the leader from time to time to test that it has not lost its touch.

**49**

Parents of teenagers are usually relieved when the teenage years have passed. It is no different with the adolescent dog. With patience and control on your part, this difficult period in your dog's life will pass smoothly. By training our dogs to be obedient we can assure ourselves of always being in control. But we will only remain in control if we constantly display consistency toward our dogs.

# Dog psychology made simple

Because so many of us own dogs today, it is essential to understand just what it is that makes a dog tick. In this section I outline the basic psychology of the dog.

A dog has many of the same basic needs that we do. It craves love and respect, companionship, food and water, and a place to belong.

A dog learns from experience. If it has a bad experience, it will remember that experience. Then, the next time, it will either be more wary or avoid altogether whatever it was that caused that experience. As we have seen, misbehavior may be the result of a bad experience.

A dog has a very good memory, which is triggered by certain scents or familiar things. Once the dog scents or sees certain items it will remember exactly what happened the last time. A dog can meet us once, and then remember months later by analysing our scent.

I once trained a dog for the stage play "Annie". Seven years later the same dog was put in the same stage play and he went through his paces, not forgetting a single thing. The first time the dog had been in this play, he had stopped to have a shake while crossing from one side of the stage to the other. As a result, every night after that he would shake at the exact same spot, for something at that point triggered the shaking response. Seven years later, in the same play, the dog shook himself at that identical place.

Dogs, like us, are creatures of habit and will continue in a set pattern unless something comes along to change it. A reprimand from another dog or its owner would create this kind of change.

Dogs do not have analytical minds as we have. A dog cannot work out the fact that it is stronger than we are. If it does this, it is only by accident. For instance, a dog on a lead could drag us down

the street without much effort, yet hundreds of dogs walk quietly at heel because they do not know their own strength.

We must also remember that a dog perceives the world in a very different way to humans. For instance, what does a dog actually see? Scientific research has shown us that the dog's eye lacks certain components found in the human eye. It is believed that because of this a dog probably sees the world in shades of black, white and grey. Other differences mean that dogs have far better night vision than humans. There can also be signifi-

cant variations between breeds. Short nosed dogs appear to have better stereoscopic sight and perception of vision that longer nosed breeds due to the positioning of their eyes, and a great many toy breeds seem to be rather short sighted.

The German police force carried out some revealing experiments in the 1950s using ten police dogs and handlers. First, they sat the men on chairs at one end of a large room and one by one they allowed the dogs into the room. Each handler would call to their dog and when it was released the dog would move

# BUDDY'S BRILLIANCE

Buddy, a two-year-old Bull Terrier, was blind. Imagine my surprise when I visited him to cure his barking problem and he and his owner began to play a game of catch. Buddy would wait facing his owner for the ball to be thrown, he would hear the ball bounce once and then pounce quickly and with amazing accuracy. With the ball in his mouth, he would bring it to the top of the hill, let it go and chase it down. You could see his concentration on the sound of the rolling ball and if he ever momentarily lost track of the ball his sense of smell would lead him to it.

directly to its handler. Then they removed all the dogs from the room and rearranged the handlers. Again the dogs were brought into the room one by one but this time they were not called. As soon as each dog was released it headed straight to the same spot that its handler had occupied the last time. When a dog found that the handler was not there, it sniffed each handler in turn until it located its master. Because all the handlers were wearing identical police uniforms and therefore looked very similar, the experiment was repeated with the handlers stripped to the waist. The results were the same.

Humans recognize each other by our features but dogs do not recognize us this way. Instead, they can identify us from the way that we walk, the sound of our voice or our individual smell.

A dog's eyesight is worse in relation to things that are static. Yet a dog will quickly see and respond to things that are moving. A dog's horizon is lower than ours, as its height is lower. So when we are walking a dog we will see many things before it does. Also, a dog will rarely look up of its own free will, unless something, such as a sound, attracts its attention. Our case study of Buddy illustrates how well a dog can function without eyesight.

Hearing is the most accutely developed sense in dogs. They have an extraordinary ability not only to notice sounds but also to identify them. A man told me how his dog slept out of sight on the back porch and would not stir if a family member entered the front yard. But immediately a stranger entered the property the dog would distinguish that this was a foreign sounding footstep and spring into action, growling and barking. He never got it wrong.

When it comes to the sense of smell the difference between dog and human capabilities is extraordinary. It is the sense that marks the greatest difference in how dogs and humans perceive the world. A dog can track a person through the woods by a scent that is days old. This ability obviously developed in the wild dogs on their hunt for prey; locating food was a matter of survival. Still, it has its limitations. Dogs cannot effectively detect scents from a distance. They must come close to us to smell us or put their nose firmly to the ground to track us. Alternately, they will lift their noses high in the air trying to pinpoint a smell on currents of air.

The sense of smell is closely linked to taste and because a dog is so sensitive it is usually smell that makes a dog reject food before it even enters its mouth. In contrast, humans have five times as many taste buds and tend to taste food before rejecting it.

Behavior is very much affected by hormones. The male hormone may be one reason why males dogs are often more playful than female dogs. Of course, this drive would combine with normal social interplay of the pack where young dogs would try out sexual advances and physical confrontations with other dogs in the pack to establish their position in the hierarchy.

More serious aggression and destructive behavior can be traced to the influence of hormones on male and female dogs. A female dog that has not been neutered (desexed) will come into season every four to six months. At that time, their whole personality can alter—as well as displaying an increased appetite, an otherwise well behaved dog may become stubborn, disobedient and preoccupied. The male dog can be much worse. Nothing is an effective deterrent to an amorous male in the pursuit of love. I knew a dog that ate its way through a fence one week and a garage door the next to get to a bitch in season! Not only does this desire to breed mean that owners may end up with litters of pups on their hands but your male dog may also be running loose on the streets, exposed to dangerous situations and possibly becoming a public nuisance. If your male dog comes across a rival, both will fight to determine who wins the girl.

One sure way of avoiding these problems is to neuter both male and female dogs at puberty (six to eight months of age). Many people are concerned that neutering will have an adverse affect their dogs' personality. I have yet to find major differences between a dog that is neutered and one that is not except that a neutered dog is less aggressive. Some put on weight due to an increased appetite. This can be controlled through a change of diet and regular exercise. Training and a bone can provide effective distractions for a dog that is no longer occupying its time thinking about sex.

Do not be alarmed if you see your puppy taking up sexual positions with other pups. This is a normal part of play which allows them to learn about physical positioning, solicitation and rejection without risk, and facilitates normal sexual functioning as an adult dog.

# Food and medication

We have concluded that not all behavioral problems have psychological cause. In fact, if your dog seems hyperactive, diet may be the reason. Prepared foodstuffs have brought many benefits to dogs and their owners by providing meals that are simple, quick and nutritionally balanced. However, as well as the vitamins and minerals that have been added to these products, there are often preservatives and chemicals and, like some humans, some dogs react adversely to them. The owners of a hyperactive dog should first try to eliminate these additives from their dog's diet to ascertain if they are in fact the reason for the dog's bad behavior.

Like humans, dogs are sometimes prescribed medication for particular behavioral problems. It should always be remembered that giving a sedative to a dog (or person) is only a temporary measure, not a cure. Medication can sometimes be useful when a dog has to be transported but the only effective way to solve the problem is through training.

## Chapter Four

# Problems and Their Cures

*In this chapter you will read about many common behavioral problems in dogs. Case studies will show how these problems arise, how the dog behaves when it has the problem, and what can be done to change the behavior. All the background information you need about techniques and tools can be found in detail in Chapter Two.*

# Noisy dogs

Dogs bark at many things. What they bark at depends on their breed and temperament. Some timid dogs will bark at anything that moves. You will find that herding dogs, such as Collies, Welsh Corgis, and Australian Cattle Dogs, will usually bark at and attack anything with wheels, such as lawn mowers, motorbikes, cars and skateboards. Terriers usually bark at people and dogs, and the same goes for Dobermanns, German Shepherds and Rottweilers. The hunting and sporting breeds are more prone than others to howling or barking when left alone. This group includes the Labradors, Retrievers, Pointers and Spaniels.

## Why do dogs bark?

Barking and growling is a dog's language. The main reason wild dogs used to bark was to warn other members of the pack about any threat. Similarly, the domesticated dog barks to alert its owner. This action of barking as a warning is the reason humans and dogs got together. Prehistoric people soon realized the benefits of having a creature around that could warn them of approaching danger.

However, in today's society we all live in close proximity to one another, and a barking dog can be more of a hindrance than a help, especially one that barks at everything that moves. People have a very low tolerance of noisy dogs. In any case, a dog that barks at everything is not a very good guard dog. It is like a car alarm that has gone berserk: no one takes an incessant alarm seriously.

Even the most vociferous of barkers can change their habits, however, if we train them correctly. It is possible to train dogs to bark only at relevant things such as intruders or visitors who enter the property unannounced, and not to respond in the same way to the mailman, the dog next door or its owners and friends.

# Curing the frequent barker

To stop a dog barking all the time, you need first of all to show it what it is doing wrong. To do this you need to gain the dog's respect by conditioning it, and then reprimand it for barking by throwing the reprimand chain on the ground near its legs. Once the barking stops, pat the dog lavishly. Keep going in this fashion until the dog ignores what it was barking at.

Dogs bark at many things. You must train yourself to react to things you *do not* want your dog to bark at and praise it for barking at the right things. Teaching the dog how to differentiate between good and bad barking will take time and effort. Reprimands given at the right time cured Zoe, the dog in the barking case study.

## ZOE'S ZEALOUS BARKING

Zoe was a German Shepherd whose frequent barking had caused her owners numerous friendships and hours of sleep. The local council had also threatened action. Her owners chose a temporary solution and gave her tranquillizers, but these just knocked her out, which was very distressing. Next they bought a sonic collar that emitted a high-pitched sound every time the dog barked. Zoe, an intelligent dog, now barked in tune with the collar's sound.

When I was called in to treat Zoe, I began by conditioning her. Then I set the scene to get her barking: a friend was to walk past the house with her dog. Zoe ran at the dog and its owner, barking, and I reprimanded her by throwing the reprimand chain at the fence in front of her. She responded, and the treatment was repeated with further scene setting.

The owners were left with instructions to continue the treatment, and after two weeks Zoe was cured. From that time onward she has learnt when she is allowed to bark and has barked only at people who enter the property unannounced.

## Howling

"The call of the wild" may be the most ingrained instinct response that a dog has, although selective breeding has seen a lot of wild instincts dominated by more sedate ones. In many cases, howling is a dog's lament when the rest of the pack (its owner and family) has left it. Others react to another dog's howl in a response that is almost a reflex, much like people yawning.

Sounds of similar pitch, like music or a siren, may set the dog howling. Using our usual reprimand techniques, the chain and the BAD word, we can train a dog to stop much of this behavior. If your dog is reacting to music—like Sonny in our case study—I also suggest that you tune your stereo to bass notes rather than higher pitches and avoid music with violins and flutes which are often pitched at a level that elicits a howling response.

## SONNY'S SENSITIVITY

Sonny, a Labrador, and his owner were the greatest of friends except for one rather annoying disagreement—Sonny did not seem to share his owner's taste in music or maybe he was too fond of it. Every time his owner put on his favorite music, Sonny would howl through the whole performance. He was about to find Sonny a whole new band to sing with. That was when I was called in.

First I conditioned Sonny to respond to the BAD word, then the owner put on his music. Sonny immediately assumed his singing position and began to howl. As we had prearranged, I had the owner throw the reprimand chain into a strategically placed metal container and yell "Bad" in a deep throated growl. Sonny was immediately distracted and jumped up to investigate. The owner then gave him a treat and a pat. After a number of repetitions, Sonny caught on to the fact that his owner was not pleased with his singing.

His owner now enjoys his music in peace (although, I will admit, every now and again those tunes are just too much for Sonny and he still has to hum along).

# Aggression

A dog that barks persistently may be a nuisance, but that does not mean it is displaying aggression. In many cases barking only means the dog is not sure of what it has spotted, and is giving a warning, rushing at the intruder and displaying bravado. When the scent of the newcomer lets the dog know that he or she poses no threat, its tail will wag: the stranger is accepted.

Aggressive behavior goes far beyond this point. Even after the dog has scented the intruder, its desire to repel still persists. This desire takes the form of snapping, snarling, and barking, accompanied by vigorous body movements. Some dogs will launch a frontal attack, while other, less confident, dogs will circle and try to go for a rear attack. In most cases, intrusion by the owner will usually be viewed as backup, and will only incite the dog and give it more confidence. The result? The dog will probably bite the stranger.

Aggression makes a dog difficult to live with, and even dangerous. You need to make your dog realize that you are not going to tolerate its aggressive behavior. Be persistent, and build the dog's respect for you. Only then should the treatment commence. However, if your problem is too difficult to solve, do not endanger either yourself or your dog. Call in an expert.

## What makes some dogs aggressive?

One of my favorite sayings is, "You can take the dog out of the wild, but you cannot take the wild out of the dog." This means simply that the dog never loses its natural instincts—its wild behavior is never far below the surface. Sometimes this behavior manifests itself as aggression.

One breed of dog is not necessarily more aggressive than any other. I have treated all breeds of dogs for aggression, and have found that the diminutive Chihuahua can be just as aggressive as the large Rottweiler or German Shepherd. The only real difference is that the larger dog can instill more fear in us because of its size.

People sometimes act in certain ways that may unconsciously encourage an aggressive attack from a dog. I knew one man whose job involved visiting many homes. On one occasion he entered a yard and was rushed by a Bull Terrier. As the dog got close the man thrust his briefcase into the dog's face, fearing an attack. Immediately the dog took hold of the bag and the man panicked, using his walking stick to hit the dog. The dog went berserk and the man was only rescued when the dog's worried owner arrived—but not before receiving 47 puncture wounds to his body. That man found out the hard way that dogs do not react well when confronted with aggression.

It is helpful to know how you should act around any animal that is prone to aggression, whether it is your dog before it is trained or strange dogs you may encounter.

Remember that dominance is not the same as aggression and you do not want to fight the dog.

A noisy dog is
an annoyance to
everybody and a
dog that barks at
everything is no
use as a watch dog
as its warnings will
be ignored.

Your dog must be
conditioned to the
BAD word before
you attempt any cure.

Use the reprimand
chain to stop the dog
barking once it is
conditioned.

*Even the mildest form of aggression should be viewed seriously. If not controlled, it can lead to vicious biting.*

*Negative behavior should be met by a negative response. Check your dog strongly and yell "Bad" followed by a quick pat when the dog responds.*

*A reprimand chain thrown very close to the dog's back legs, accompanied by a forceful use of the BAD word, will work effectively with most dogs.*

Bone burying may be one reason behind destructive digging but often the key is boredom—and the more intelligent the dog, the bigger the problem.

Chewing can be a very expensive problem, particularly if your dog has taken a liking to your furniture. Hot chili or curry sauce painted on your possessions should deter even the most determined dog.

To discourage the hole-digger place some of the dog's droppings in the freshly dug hole.

Some dogs will steal anything the moment your back is turned.

Theft can turn into an even bigger problem if your dog becomes aggressive and tries to stop you from retrieving your property.

A reprimand chain thrown near your dog or an atomizer sprayed in its face, along with the BAD word, will soon cure the kleptomaniac.

Remember how dogs act with each other, how they display their dominance through a stiff, upright stance.

Remember as well that dogs are attracted by movement. Making quick moves or running could be perceived by the dog as a threat of attack. Remember that a dog's eyesight is not good for detail at a distance. Stand very still and give the dog time to assess who has walked into their territory and what that person wants.

Whatever its breed, a dog with aggressive behavior has a complex behavioral problem. It may be showing any one of many different types of aggression: fear aggression; control aggression; overprotectiveness; aggression that is purpose-trained; food aggression; predatory aggression toward other animals; and aggression to other dogs.

I will examine each of these types of aggression in turn, and show ways of handling dogs with this behavior. Fear aggression will be dealt with last, because the case study of a fearful dog can be better understood once you know more about the other forms of aggression.

But in our first case study on aggression we look at Hans and how my reaction to his attacks made all the difference.

# Control aggression

This is probably the most basic form of aggression found among dogs. Humans can control others with words or with actions. The dog does not have words at its disposal. Its way of communicating is simple: growling and barking, and with body language. It uses growling as a warning, that may be quickly followed by a bite if there is no response to it.

A lot of dogs use control aggression to get their own way. Being a pack animal, the dog still operates according to pack laws, and will test the pack leader to see if it is still dominant. A domesticated dog will test the owner, who is its pack leader. If it seems you have lost control as the leader, the dog will display aggression toward you, showing its lack of respect—it will snap and growl to prevent you from doing things such as taking food from it, picking it up, bathing it, or moving it.

To prevent control aggression in our dogs, we need to be consistent at all times, and we need to establish our pack leadership firmly with our dogs by conditioning them daily. When we condition a dog we leave it in no doubt that we are the leader of the pack.

# HANS' HOSTILITY

Hans was a two-year-old German Shepherd who already had a criminal record when I was called in to help him. Over a three month period, he had bitten five people. The final victim had reported Hans to the police but had agreed not to prosecute if Hans received therapy and training. When I arrived at the property, I was met by a ferocious dog that I assumed was my pupil.

This dog lunged at me the moment I alighted from my car. I stood my ground, however, without flinching. He stopped short, waiting for me to make a move, then backed away uncertainly. I took another step forward and he lunged again, this time more aggressively. I stood firmly again and yelled "Bad". Again he backed off, further this time, still growling and barking but not game to launch another attack.

Just then the owner arrived. He had been delayed in traffic and was amazed to find that I had not been bitten by Hans. I explained my technique. Most people will run away, back down or kick out to defend themselves from a dog's attack. This only incites the dog to further aggression. The reason I had not been bitten was that I had sent Hans signals that confused him. He could not establish from my actions whether I was frightened of him or whether I posed a threat as my body language neither confirmed or denied these possibilities.

As Hans' owner put him on a lead to begin our therapy, he received a phone call relaying that a worker had been bitten by Hans earlier that morning, about 15 minutes before I arrived. That man was now in hospital receiving treatment.

So how did we rehabilitate Hans? First his owner built a secure pen to protect Hans and people from the dog's unsociable behavior. The pen also allowed us to establish a controlled situation because I wanted the owner to reprimand Hans every time he showed aggression to anybody. The only safe way to do this was to have the dog in a pen.

## Overprotectiveness

Dogs have a natural instinct of protectiveness, which can take many forms. They will protect their owners the way they would protect the pack leader, and they also will protect the owner's possessions, because dogs see them as the pack's possessions.

Cars, for example, can make dogs overprotective just because they are compact and enclosed. In such a small area a dog·can feel threatened: it feels cornered, as there seems to be no way out. To solve this problem, replace the dog's anxiety by giving it something to anticipate. Food can be used to distract the dog: usually all it takes to control some dogs is to have strangers to the dog approach the car and drop food in through a partially opened window.

For the dog that cannot be won over with food, discipline and control will have to be used: in other words, reprimanding. When the dog is in the car, place a receptacle in the car that will amplify sound, such as a large cooking pot. Leave a window slightly open so you can reach the receptacle easily. Have a stranger to your dog approach the car it is protecting. Stay hidden, appearing only when the dog barks or growls, and throw the reprimand chain into the receptacle, yelling the BAD word at the very moment the dog displays aggression. The cooking pot will magnify the sound of the chain, and the dog will see the sound as a signal to stop its barking. Pat or praise the dog the instant it responds positively.

Some dogs are overprotective of their owners and their homes and may act aggressively toward strangers. The best way to solve this type of aggression is to condition the dog. Then ask a friend who is a stranger to the dog to visit your house to help you. Place the dog on a lead, but leave the lead on the ground rather than holding it in your hand, and plant your foot firmly on the lead. Make yourself a reprimand chain, or use a can half filled with pebbles. This will be used to create a diversion when your helper knocks at the door. Throw the can or chain on the floor near the dog at the precise second the dog becomes aggressive, stepping on the lead at the same time. Alternatively, another friend (who the dog knows and respects) could hold the lead loosely until the dog becomes aggressive, then snap the lead back as you throw the can or chain on the floor. This scenario will need to be repeated several times, with different helpers. If treatment proves too difficult, seek professional help. Some dogs will need an expert.

Maternal aggression is perhaps the most instinctive form of protectiveness. In the wild, the pups were prone to attack from other dogs who saw the new members as a potential threat to their position. This behavior may be particularly strong with the birth of a first litter but in all cases it will diminish as the pups mature.

# Trained aggression

Sometimes the aggressive behavior of a dog is a direct response to the actions of the owner. A dog may have become aggressive because its owner inadvertently did the wrong thing by patting and soothing it when it acted aggressively. Such action by the owner only increases the dog's aggression, as it feels it is being supported in its behavior.

Also, with the increase of crime in today's society, many people seek professional training for their dogs to make them aggressive to strangers and more protective of their owners and their possessions. A dog that is trained to be aggressive has simply had its natural protective instincts finely tuned and strengthened by training. This type of dog could be dangerous in the wrong hands; it could be suspicious of everyone, and act aggressively toward anyone it encounters. As dogs do not possess a conscience, the owner needs to be fully in control at all times. Whatever the origins of your dog's trained aggression, you can try to control it by conditioning and reprimanding. If you believe your dog may be too dangerous to handle, you may have to call in an expert.

# Food protection and aggression

This is one of the most natural forms of aggression. A dog in the wild has stiff competition over food from other pack members, and guards its own food carefully. The instinct of the dog, both wild and domesticated, is self-preservation, and it will drive off any dog or human who might try to take its food away. Owners may find this distressing: they give the dog its food, yet it shows aggression toward them each time they approach while it is eating.

Not all dogs have to be hostile food guarders, however. Some, with proper handling from puppyhood, have learnt no reason to fear anyone approaching their food. You can achieve this with your overprotective dog with conditioning —making the dog realize that when you take food away it will always be given back.

To do this, play a game where the dog is always the winner. Place it on its lead at feeding time, and, keeping hold of the lead, put the food on the ground. Bend down as if to take the food, and reprimand the dog if it growls, lifting it with the lead at the same time. Each time the dog growls or snaps it should be lifted and reprimanded with the BAD word, spoken in a harsh growl. As soon as the dog stops being aggressive, that is, it stops growling or snapping, return the food to it.

A dog that refuses to yield will probably need an expert. Seek professional advice if your dog proves too difficult for you to deal with yourself.

A dog that is overly aggressive with its food should not be given bones, at least not until it is cured, otherwise the bone could be buried by the dog. This is a potentially dangerous situation. Anyone accidentally digging the bone up could be attacked by the dog.

# Aggression toward other dogs

Dogs in the wild would drive off any other dog or any marauding animal that approached the pack or their territory. Today many owners expect their dogs to behave in a friendly way to all other dogs that come along, but some individual dogs, and some breeds, have a stronger instinct to protect the pack than others. I have found that German Shepherds, Greyhounds, Welsh Corgis, Australian Cattle Dogs, Rottweilers, and Terriers of all kinds, have a very strong pack instinct which can be both a good and problematic trait.

The early socialization of a dog is paramount if it is to establish good relations with other dogs. Chapter Three's section on "A Well-adjusted Puppy" deals with this topic in more detail. Neutering can also be beneficial in this regard as an adjunct to the training, but is recommended at an early age—about six months.

A submissive dog may never have a problem when dealing with other dogs, choosing instead to show immediately that it is no threat by squirming or grovelling, holding its tail down or between its legs, averting its eyes and pulling its ears back or flat against the head. Other dogs will immediately look for signs to establish which animal will win dominance: the stronger character will hold its tail high over its back, stand as straight and tall as it can and move with a definite, rigid gait.

Aggression toward other dogs may mean the dog pulls at its lead, trying to engage in battle with the other dog, or runs up and down behind the fence barking and growling at another dog passing by.

To gain the upper hand, you must first have well and truly established leadership over your dog. Conditioning should be carried out for at least two weeks before any attempt is made to control the dog's aggression. Only after the dog is obeying you as a result of the conditioning can effective treatment be administered.

Treatment must be conducted in a controlled environment, such as your own backyard. Have a friend walk another dog up and down the other side of the fence. Let your dog run free in your yard, with no lead on. Have a reprimand chain ready, and when the dog behaves aggressively toward the other dog, throw the chain near its hind legs and yell the BAD word as the chain lands on the ground.

The treatment will have to be repeated over a couple of weeks; throw the chain five or six times each session. Make sure the dog is cured before attempting the same thing out in the street. When you do treat the dog outside your home, make sure it is on a lead and remember that you will have to be very aggressive in your reprimand if you are to win the attention of the combative dogs away from each other.

## Predatory aggression

The hunting instinct is basic to the wild dog's survival. So when your domestic dog displays predatory aggression by going after a pet rabbit or cat it does not mean that the dog has turned savage; it is, in fact, acting in a very natural manner. There is no basis to the idea that once a dog has "tasted blood" it will attack relentlessly. A wild dog did not attack the members of its pack when it returned from the hunt. Feeding a dog raw meat or bones does not predispose it to attack. Like other forms of aggression, predatory attacks can be controlled with concentrated training.

Prevention is, as always, the best defence. Always place a young dog

on a lead when it is around other animals and teach it respect from an early and impressionable age. The same technique can be used on older dogs. A muzzle may be necessary for a dog that is very difficult to handle. As an owner, you should show strong disapproval for predatory behavior. You may need to throw a reprimand chain or can to distract the dog, yelling "Bad" at the same time and praising the dog as soon as it stops misbehaving. You will probably have to repeat these actions several times before your dog learns to ignore other animals.

See the section "Meeting other animals" in Chapter Two.

## Fear aggression

Fear is born of the unknown. The dog fears what it cannot understand or recognize as normal. For example, a dog that has been isolated from the outside world will become fearful of any unknown environment. Aggression will manifest itself in the form of driving off the unknown intruder or objects. Once the object of the dog's aggression has gone, the dog will view this as a victory and will become more and more aggressive each time, being convinced that its actions are removing of the object of its fear. That is why dogs will continue to

# WINSTON'S WARINESS

Winston, a two-year-old Border Collie, was playing a game of fetch-the-stick with his owner. When the dog pounced on the stick and screamed in pain, his owner was concerned, so she took him to the local veterinarian.

The veterinarian diagnosed soft palate damage, and put Winston on a course of antibiotics. But after a few days Winston's behavior began to puzzle his owner. He began acting strangely, like a dog suffering from paranoia.

He showed signs of agitation, and would vacate any room his owner entered, finally hiding under her bed, and refusing to budge. He even snapped and snarled at her if she attempted to move him.

Everyone the owner consulted at this point advised her to have Winston put down. They suggested that his behavior was the result of his bad experience with the stick, which he associated with her, and all felt this behavior was irreversible. But this solution was very distressing, and would have proved impossible anyway. Winston was so aggressive by now that no one the owner approached for help would come near him.

When I was called in, I joined Winston under the bed. I noticed that his eyes were wild yet glazed, and he appeared to be holding his head slightly to one side. I failed to lasso him with a lead I had, but I managed to propel him into the bathroom and into a cage. He seemed grateful for the haven it provided.

I was convinced by now that Winston was a special case: a physical problem was at the root of his fears. And this proved to be so. A long examination, during which my veterinarian and I had to wrestle with Winston and finally anesthetize him, revealed a two inch (50 mm) stick, lodged deep in his throat.

Removing the stick did not solve all of Winston's problems. He was still suffering from paranoia: his injury had made him afraid of leads, cars, vets, and strangers.

Winston remained at the veterinary hospital and I instructed the nurses not to feed him. I wanted to be the only one to do so, to build up his trust in me, so I could administer therapy.

For two days I sat in his hospital cage with him and hand-fed him, so that he began to trust me. Soon he was happy to go for walks with me, and I took him on plenty of car rides to different locations. We also visited the veterinarian many times, simply to buy doggy treats. He was then returned to his owner with instructions to continue this therapy for a few weeks.

Winston is now fully recovered, his old fearless self.

chase cars—they appear to drive away in defeat. Perhaps, as was the sad case with Jedda, the dog has experienced a trauma in the past and is now projecting that fear in other circumstances.

We have dealt with various kinds of aggression, and their causes. In each situation we have looked at aggressive behavior that was fairly long term before it was treated. But a situation may also arise where a dog that is normally happy and outgoing suddenly becomes aggressive without any obvious reason. Such a case came to my attention recently, and seemed to me a clear form of fear aggression. The story of Winston shows that in some instances a dog seems to suddenly develop a fear that then turns into paranoia. This paranoia may then manifest itself as extreme aggression toward anything that may be associated with the fear in the first place.

# Destructive chewing and digging

Today, more dogs are chewing forbidden objects, and digging up and destroying their backyards. These are forms of destructive behavior that turn the dogs into a liability to their owners. Some dogs can be a one-creature demolition team, moving insatiably from one object to the next, seemingly hellbent on destroying everything in their path.

## JEDDA'S JITTERS

A 12-month-old Mastiff named Jedda learned very early in life to be aggressive to strangers. It began when she was only six months old and her owner took her to a local show where a well-meaning exhibitor gave Jedda's new owner some disastrous advice. The woman showed the owner how to "cure" Jedda's timidness by smacking the pup every time she sulked. The result was a pup whose first introduction to strangers was physical abuse. No wonder Jedda's reaction to strangers changed from withdrawal to aggression.

After therapy, I prescribed conditioning for Jedda so that the owner regained some control of her. This was important because, to show her that people meant her no harm, we needed to take Jedda back to the scene of the crime ... dog shows. The process would take some time as her trust had to be rebuilt. First we had to walk Jedda around the perimeter of the show then gradually introduce her more closely to strangers, keeping her muzzled at the early stages for safety's sake.

I believe there is a connection between a dog's intelligence and its destructive behavior. Hyperactive children are often located in the higher intelligence bracket, and a large percentage of dogs I have treated for destructive behavior have proved to be very intelligent animals. Of course, there are other factors that promote destructive behavior, such as boredom, stress, lack of adequate housing, and lack of purpose. However, I have seen dogs of lower intelligence forced to live in these circumstances, and they have not been destructive.

I have also discovered that there are some breeds of dogs that are more prone to chewing and digging than others. Many larger breeds, such as Collies, Labradors, and German Shepherds are likely to have such problems. Australian Cattle Dogs, Poodles, and Terriers head the list for the smaller dogs.

The case study tells the story of Klint, whose lack of stimulation led to destructive behavior of this kind.

# KLINT'S COMEBACK

Klint was a two-year-old German Shepherd. His owner was reluctantly seeking a new home for him, because Klint's destructive chewing had cost him hundreds of dollars so far. The most recent calamity had been Klint's destruction of the entire interior of his owner's brand-new Volvo.

The owner told me that Klint was very well behaved, and did not bark. He had not trained the dog, convinced that Klint's good behavior made this unnecessary. Digging and chewing were his only behavioral problems, but these were becoming too expensive.

A meeting with Klint and his owner convinced me that the dog's problem was a lack of training. He was far too intelligent to go through life without any outlet for his intellect. He was bored, and that was why he chewed: he needed to be active.

I showed the owner how to condition Klint, and set a daily regime that was tailored to his busy schedule. This meant a 20-minute training procedure that included assorted obedience exercises such as getting the dog to sit, stay, and drop stay (to lie down with its forelegs stretched out on the ground, not upright, as in a sit position). The dog would also have a disciplined walk every day, which would mean making him walk at the owner's pace without tree sniffing. I wanted Klint to use his brain, not just to amble.

I also suggested that a secure pen should be erected. This would ensure no chewing would take place while we were waiting for the treatment to work. The cost of the pen would soon be offset by the absence of destructive chewing.

Four weeks after treatment commenced, I heard that the pen had stopped Klint's destructiveness immediately. He was now being let out of the pen, and was not chewing any more. He loved the training, and seemed to be a lot happier. His quick intelligence was now being challenged.

# Kleptomania

"An irresistible urge to steal" is the actual dictionary definition of kleptomania. When a dog steals objects it does not really need, we call this kleptomania, but we must be aware that the dog is not really stealing, not in the true sense of the word. A dog does not possess a conscience, and does not know it is taking away something that doesn't belong to it.

Rather, it is showing signs of possessiveness, and displaying its opportunistic nature. When it sees something it wants, it merely seizes the opportunity to grab it and possess it for itself. The "stolen" item can be any item the dog feels it wants to own—a shoe, a bone, your wallet, an article of clothing.

Most dogs give up what they snatch fairly easily, without much objection, and mostly this behavior is viewed with amusement—"The lace mats are missing, check Fido's bed again!" However, when the kleptomanic dog becomes aggressive at attempts to retrieve the missing item, the whole situation becomes far more serious. A cure must be implemented.

To control this type of problem, we need to show the dog that we are dominant. In Cleo's case study, apprehension made her owners ineffectual at controlling her stealing or regaining their property.

Note, though, that Cleo was relatively easy to handle. Some very aggressive resistance from an over-possessive kleptomaniac might need a more aggressive, confident approach. Use the conditioning treatment that we described in Chapter Two, the same as that used for Cleo, and the lead. Throw the reprimand chain near the dog at the exact second it snaps or growls, and pat or voice-praise it when it relents.

A very difficult dog might require an expert. Do not put yourself at risk with an overly aggressive dog, and consider the welfare of the dog at all times.

# Schizophrenia

This term is sometimes used by owners to describe temporary bouts of strange behavior on the part of their otherwise normal dogs. Yet there is no proof that dogs do suffer from schizophrenia. I have yet to find a true case of the complaint.

I have found that most cases I have been called in to treat had a different source.

# CLEO'S KLEPTOMANIA

Cleo was a five-year-old female Old English Sheepdog cross. She would snatch things that were either dropped or left lying around and would fiercely repel any attempts by her owners, a family of three, to get their possessions back. She would fly under the bed and snap and growl at them when their hands reached under the bed.

The owners had been trying unsuccessfully for over a year to cure their dog's kleptomania and her aggressive behavior. They were desperate to have a normal, well-adjusted dog once more. Neutering had been suggested as a solution, but as Cleo was female this was not guaranteed to work.

Cleo proved to be a friendly, loving dog, who allowed me to do anything at all to her. I dropped articles, allowed her to take them to her lair under the bed, and calmly retrieved them. She offered no resistance.

Her amazed owners then showed me how they went about getting their possessions back. They would thrust their hands under the bed and withdraw them quickly. It took only a growl or snap from the dog to deter them. Their whole approach was one of apprehension. Their technique was, in fact, had the effect of making the dog think she had the upper hand.

I prescribed some conditioning for a week before attempting treatment. Then I suggested that the owners place her on a check chain and strong webbing lead. This way they would have less resistance once the conditioning had established their leadership. They would also have a lead to assist them if they met any resistance—it could restrain the dog if she launched an attack.

This treatment was followed, and the family and their dog are much more at ease. It only took a little discipline and now Cleo is no longer a kleptomaniac.

# CLYDE'S CONSTERNATION

Clyde was a three-year-old purebred Airedale Terrier. He had always been a very happy, loving, outgoing dog everyone adored. However, in the past two years he had been behaving strangely toward owners and strangers alike. One moment he would be perfectly normal, and the next his eyes would glaze over, and he would go to his bed and sit there as if in a trance.

I asked the owner whether there was any one element always present when this happened, such as a sound or an object. Did Clyde behave strangely at night or during the day, or was a television set, washing machine or some other appliance switched on when the strange behavior was shown? It turned out that Clyde only went into his trance in the evenings, while his owners were watching television.

I had a strong feeling that something traumatic had happened to the dog during a program that was on regularly, or during a television commercial. Perhaps something fell on it, or it trod on something and hurt itself. Then it began to associate this traumatic experience with the sound it heard at the time. Whenever it subsequently heard the same sound, it would expect the trauma to recur. It would become very concerned, retreating to its bed where it felt safe, but lying there worrying until the sound passed. Then it would return to normal.

I suggested the owner should try to predict when this behavior was going to occur, by monitoring exactly what was happening when Clyde became strange. Then she should place him on a lead whenever she knew this was going to happen. As he started running toward his bed, she could use the lead to prevent his retreat. She could keep him with her, patting and consoling him and assuring him that the bad thing would not happen.

Once he realized that nothing bad had happened for some time, Clyde would soon return to normal. And that is what did happen under the protective leadership of his owner.

Supposed schizophrenia usually involves a lack of proper discipline and social structure in the dog's home, rather than any internal disorder on the part of the dog.

I was once called on to treat a crossbred Labrador/German Shepherd for a personality disorder. I noticed that the dog did not appear normal at all. Its head was held at an angle, its reflexes were slow and it appeared to walk as if drunk. I instructed the owner to take the dog to the veterinarian immediately. It was found to be suffering brain damage, probably the result of a case of mild distemper, and not a psychological disorder afterall. Unfortunately, the dog had to be put to sleep.

In the case study, it was in fact a traumatic incident that affected the personality of Clyde. The owner, who had approached me at a lecture I was giving on dog psychology, had been convinced that Clyde was schizophrenic.

# Shyness

Many of our personality traits are inherited from our parents, or relatives in previous generations. This is the same with dogs. A shy dog may well have a shy predecessor.

Lack of confidence is another factor that may make your dog shy of both strangers and people it knows well. This lack of confidence may often be attributed to a lack of socialization. If the dog was not taken to meet people and other dogs, it could very easily find them threatening.

Over-friendly people can also terrify the shy dog. Complete strangers rush at my dogs when I am walking them, and hug and pat the dogs. It is just as well that my dogs are both well adjusted; you could imagine how a shy dog would find this behavior difficult to deal with. I often wonder how the same people would cope if a complete stranger came rushing up to them in the street and then began to kiss and cuddle them. I maintain that they would be quite perturbed.

The shy dog may have suffered a trauma early in its life—it may have been treated badly by a stranger or another dog. I quite regularly hear horror stories from clients about the things that have happened to their dogs at the hands of other people. Regal's case study is the story of a dog that became overly shy after suffering two separate traumatic experiences at the hands of thoughtless people.

# REGAL'S RETICENCE

Regal was a shy Scottish Collie whom I was called in to treat for excessive barking. This misbehavior was caused by her fear of strangers. This fear in turn had arisen from two traumatic experiences she had had as a young, very impressionable puppy of about three months.

The first trauma occurred when her owner took her to visit with friends. A friend of the owner's picked the puppy up and literally threw it across the room to someone else.

If that wasn't enough, it was only a short time after that another friend of the owner's visited her home. As he entered, Regal barked at the stranger. The visitor ran at the pup and chased her through the house, imitating the way she was barking, until eventually poor Regal ended up a shivering wreck in the corner, wetting herself with fright.

As a result of these two experiences, Regal not only became very shy of strangers but this shyness also resulted in the dog barking frantically at them, hoping they would run away and leave her alone and safe.

The treatment I prescribed was some conditioning for about a week, followed by some "stranger desensitization". This meant having strangers visit the house on a regular basis so that the dog's confidence in strangers could be rebuilt. I stressed that Regal's owner would have to be very selective in her choice of friends to help her rehabilitate her dog.

I also asked Regal's owner to reprimand the dog each time she barked, using the reprimand chain. She was to throw it on the ground near the dog's back legs and yell "Bad!", praising her with vigorous patting as soon as she stopped misbehaving. My reason for the strong reprimand in this case was to make a forcible change to Regal's habits. If a shy dog has a barking problem in addition to the problem of its shyness, its fear is usually very difficult to overcome.

Tying up a dog or leaving it alone for long hours can create a lot of stress which may, in turn, lead to destructive behavior and barking.

Throwing a ball for your dog is a great stress reliever—for both of you! But throwing a stick may be dangerous as it can get caught in your dog's throat or injure its eyes.

A dog that leads an active life is less likely to suffer stress. Remember that spending time with your dog is essential to its wellbeing.

Dogs that chase stock, bicycles and cars are a danger to themselves and others.

Attach a long lead to your dog's collar or check chain to control chasing.

By checking the dog when it is actually chasing something we can eventually have control both on and off the lead. Use the BAD word as the dog is checked backward.

A dog that charges ahead tugging you along makes the walk not only miserable for its owner but also uncomfortable for itself.

The correct way to fit a check chain is with the dog on your left. Be sure that the section attached to the lead comes over your dog's neck, not under its chin. The chain should check and release easily.

DO NOT bend your arm when using the check chain. You will just be lifting the weight of the dog.

*DO keep the dog to your left and your left arm stiff. Snap the lead in one motion. First move your arm forward to release the lead, then snap back sharply and bring your arm quickly back to its starting position.*

*The lead should always be held loosely and only snapped back quickly when the dog is out of position. Say "Bad" when you snap the lead and praise your dog when it is level with your legs.*

*Praise is one of the most important parts of training. Never hold back praise for good behavior even if your dog has previously made you angry. Always pat your dog at the exact instant it obeys you and you will see the good results.*

# Nervousness

A nervous dog is a dog that stands shaking and shivering each time it hears a loud noise or is confronted with something it does not understand. Like the shy dog, the nervous dog likely to have inherited its temperament. It may have suffered a trauma that has made it a nervous dog, but this is unlikely. A dog with a nervous disorder was usually born with this disorder.

There are certain things we can do to improve the quality of life for the nervous dog. A daily dose of vitamin B—approximately 3 oz (100 gm) is recommended—could improve the nervous system, but will only really work on the dog that is vitamin B deficient. You will only notice a difference after about three months, and there may in fact be no improvement.

You could also take a look at your dog's diet. There may be chemicals, like preservatives, in the dog foods it eats; these additives can sometimes be toxic to the dog, causing allergies that can affect its nervous system.

The nervous dog is very difficult to deal with and train, as its nervousness will override everything else. A nervous dog running for its life from a threatening situation is very hard to stop, and it may even nip or bite if cornered. The best way to deal with this type of dog is to be very firm. You will have to be in control at all times.

Socialization will not change this dog's fears. It will have to be forced to live with those things that frighten it. You will have to take it back again and again to the things that unnerve it. This will help a little, and should improve the dog's behavior slightly. I am yet to find a truly nervous dog that could be completely rehabilitated, but even a slight improvement makes life easier for both the dog and its owner, as it did in Renae's case.

# Fussy eaters

Because food is plentiful in the world of today's domestic dog, the urgency of the dog to find and eat food is not a strong instinct. The dog's ancestors, on the other hand, had to hunt to survive. They would hunt in packs, mainly surviving on small rodents, injured or weak grazing animals, berries, or scavenging. Wild dogs, given the opportunity, would eat almost anything that came their way.

# RENAE'S REHABILITATION

Renae was a two-year-old Poodle. He had his owner, a doctor, near exhaustion with his nervous behavior. The owner liked to entertain a lot, and wanted his dog to enjoy the regular visitors to the home. All Renae would do was run upstairs and hide every time a stranger arrived. If the owner sat and cuddled the dog when a visitor was there, it would shake and growl throughout the visit, barking frantically whenever the visitor stood up or moved around.

When I met Renae, he refused to let me touch him and gave the odd snap. After observing him, I diagnosed him as a very nervous dog. He needed better communication with his owner, so that he could realize his behavior was not approved of. His undesirable behavior should be discouraged, and his good behavior should be rewarded.

I had his owner place a check chain and lead on him. This way I had control of the dog, he could not run away, and I could handle him without his being able to nip me. He needed to be reprimanded for his bad behavior with the BAD word and the chain, and praised for good, desirable behavior. I conditioned him to teach him right from wrong, using the BAD word every time he moved. Nervous dogs need their owners to be fairly tough, otherwise they will continue to do whatever they feel saves them from confrontation with the enemy.

In time, Renae let me walk around him, and responded to the reprimand word. Once I had completed the conditioning, we called in a friend to act as a visitor. We had attached a light lead to prevent Renae's retreat. I instructed the owner to use the BAD word each time the dog barked or tried to run upstairs.

With continued training Renae's behavior did improve. He never fully accepted people, but at least he did not bark at them or run away. This meant he was less stressed—and so were his owner and the visitors.

How the dog's ancestors would have loved being able to scratch at the back door or carry their bowls in to their owners! Today, when our dogs do this, we simply open a can or slice a piece of meat off a sausage and place it in their bowls. No wonder we have fussy eaters.

Many dog owners spoil their dogs by tempting them with many different varieties of food until they accept one and eat it, only to refuse it after a few months. Then the search goes on to find something the dog will eat.

Admittedly, dogs do need variety. Eating the same things can be boring, and, after all, the dog's ancestors had plenty of variety in the wild. The problem is some dogs, like some children, will not always eat what is good for them and as a result can suffer from mineral and vitamin deficiencies. Thankfully, like Pebbles in our case study, dogs can be trained to eat normally.

# PEBBLES' POOR DIET

Pebbles was a 12-month-old Shih Tzu. Her fussy eating had her owners in a quandary. They had gone the "tempt-her-with-anything" road, but they were becoming increasingly concerned at the lack of vitamins and minerals in her diet. Pebbles would eat nothing but cooked ground beef. She had been weaned on it, and although sometimes she would nibble on some other dog food, she would always return to it.

Pebbles' problem was that she had been weaned on insufficiently nutrient-rich food. Her taste buds were conditioned to eating that food. If her diet were to continue, deficiencies would occur, followed by illness, bone deformities or worse.

I instructed her owners to choose a dog food alternative that was nutritionally well-balanced. The food they selected or prepared had to contain protein, cereals and vitamin C. These nutrients could be found in meat, cooked brown rice, offal (food like kidney, liver and heart), and cooked vegetables. This would match the diet of a dog in the wild, which would devour a whole animal: the meat, the offal, the bones, and even the stomach contents, which included cereal or vegetable matter.

The owners were told they should now give Pebbles only a half portion of her ground beef. The other half should be the balanced food. Over the next few weeks they should continue reducing the proportion of beef in relation to the other food until she was having a balanced diet. If, at any time during the transition or afterwards, she refused to eat the balanced food, they should cover her dish with plastic wrap, keep it in the fridge and go on offering it to her until she ate it. They would have to be tough with their dog in order to correct her bad eating habits, but she would not starve herself to death. I have used this method many times to correct fussy eaters.

Pebbles went on to become a normal eater, and will now eat anything her owners give her.

## TYSON'S TROUBLES

Tyson was an eight-month-old German Shepherd. His sexual indiscretions were proving difficult: he was constantly riding the legs of his owners and their guests.

When I met Tyson, he proceeded to ride my leg. His owners said, "Feel privileged—he likes you." I could see that Tyson's sexual advances were his way of controlling people, his way of dominating them. No one was game enough to reprimand him for his indiscretions.

My first object was to establish a rapport between myself and the dog. I offered him doggy treats, and then took him for a walk around the block myself, to make him responsive to my instructions.

When we returned from the walk, I took him into the yard and began conditioning him to the BAD word. Once he was conditioned, I told the owners to keep doing this for five minutes each day. They should use the BAD word each time he tried his sexual advances, and then give him a doggy treat immediately when he ceased.

It took Tyson's owners only two weeks of repeated training to cure his problem completely.

# Sexual etiquette

Dogs think mostly of two things— food and sex. An oversexed dog can be a real nuisance, and a danger to our children. Young dogs are often the worst offenders, as the hormones in their young bodies are developing the male sex hormone (testosterone) or the female sex hormone (estrogen). Because of the surge of the hormones in the developing dog, their sexual responses can sometimes be directed at the wrong target—at children, stuffed toys, blankets or adults' legs. Male dogs are the worst offenders, but many female dogs have the same problem.

# CHANTEL'S SHAME

Chantel was an 18-month-old Standard Poodle. She was left alone a lot while her owners were at work. So great was the stress she suffered that the backyard would look like a disaster area when her owners returned each evening—she was eating her way through their wooden garden furniture and verandah. They would show her what she had done wrong, and hit her with a rolled-up newspaper. This only made her chew more, and they were considering getting rid of her.

When I met Chantel she seemed very agitated, darting from one place to another. The owners were convinced that she knew she had done wrong. They pointed to the chewed garden setting and said, "Who did this?" The dog immediately put her ears back, cringing.

I explained that a dog has no concept of right or wrong, no memory of what it has done. The only way to teach it something is wrong is to catch it in the act, and reprimand it immediately. I called Chantel to me, took her by the collar, and led her to the garden shed. I pointed to the door, which was in perfect condition.

"Who did this?" I asked. Chantel immediately cringed. She knew I was angry, but not what I was angry about.

I instructed the owners to condition their dog to the BAD word and use that as a reprimand. They should also pretend to leave, and then sneak back in and reprimand Chantel in the act of chewing. This would make her think that they were always there, and reduce its stress. Also, to protect their wooden furniture and verandah, they should paint them with hot chili sauce.

A week later, Chantel was far more relaxed. The furniture had suffered no further destruction. Her owners had given her toys and old bits of wood to chew. They had caught her chewing a couple of times by sneaking back when she thought they were out. Now they had finally thrown the newspaper away.

Neutering is one way of stopping this problem rather quickly, and the ideal age to neuter a dog is at six months. Your other option is to train your dog to have decent sexual etiquette, as I did with Tyson in the case study.

## Stress

A dog that constantly chews, howls or digs may be a stressed dog. This stress may arise if the dog is left alone at home. In a pack situation, a dog would almost always accompany the rest of the pack when they went hunting. So when we leave our dogs alone they cannot understand why they cannot accompany the other members of the pack, in this case their owners. We may have taken this pack animal from its mother and litter as a small puppy. Then we put it into our yard, and turned it into a solitary animal with little or no contact with other dogs or people.

The ideal situation is to have two dogs. This way the dog will have company while we are away for long hours at the office, school or the supermarket. Some people, however, have no desire to own two dogs, and would prefer to solve the problem of their dog's stress in another way. One such couple were the owners of Chantel in our case study.

## Chasing

It is a very natural thing for a dog to chase anything that moves. This instinct is probably what made the dog's ancestors first realize that they could catch their own food. So the instinct to chase is governed by the instinct to survive. Today a dog will chase small animals such as rabbits and rodents, and also other dogs, bicycles, vehicles, sheep, and cattle.

Although chasing is an inherent instinct, a dog can be trained not to chase. I believe all dogs should be discouraged from chasing, unless of course you have a racing Greyhound.

It is better to train a dog not to chase when it is young, preferably in the first 12 months of its life, as at this age it is too young to have established strong behavior patterns. I always start training a puppy not to chase from the very first week I bring it home. I introduce it to my other dogs and pets and teach the newcomer to respect them. I take the pup with me when I go out, and attach a long lightweight lead to correct any early chasing. I simply tug on the lead and yell "Bad" any time the pup shows too much interest in any other animals, vehicles or bicycles. I also choose a deserted field or street, and have a friend drive a car and then ride a bicycle up and down past the pup. Again I reprimand the pup each time it runs at the vehicle or bicycle. There may be three to four weeks of long lead training before you can trust the dog off the lead.

Solving this problem is slightly more difficult with the older dog, as in most cases it will have been chasing for quite some time—and enjoying it. The cure will need to be very dramatic and forceful, as in the case study of Dougal.

It is important to ensure that your dog respects the person who helps you train it not to chase. Only through respect will a dog accept the reprimand without becoming aggressive.

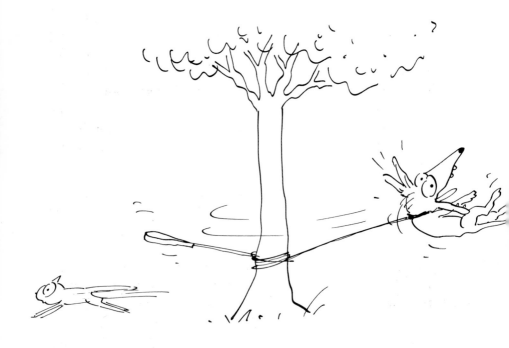

## DOUGAL'S DARING

Dougal, a five-year-old Border Collie, was a chronic chaser, and had been like this since he was a young puppy. When I met him, he was frantically running after the chickens in a coop. When his owner managed to stop him, he went after a cat instead, and then a car was his next target.

To treat Dougal, I first conditioned him, and then armed the owner of the chickens with a reprimand chain and instructed him to stay well hidden until the dog was almost at the coop. I attached a long lightweight lead to Dougal.

Dougal ran happily toward the coop. I gave him lots of rope, as I did not want him to know he was on a lead. Just as he ran at the chickens, their owner popped out from behind a tree and threw the reprimand chain, loudly yelling the BAD word. It landed on the ground just in front of Dougal as he was running. He stopped in his tracks and ran back to me. I praised him lavishly. I tried to walk him back toward the chickens again, but he flatly refused. We repeated the action with the lead and the hidden person with chain for all the things Dougal normally chased, including vehicles.

Dougal's owner had to continue the therapy. It took a month of follow-up by his owner, but after that Dougal never chased another thing.

# Walking problems

Dogs are natural pullers. Think of the sled dogs in Alaska that enjoy pulling sleds. Regardless of what restraint we attach to a dog's neck, the dog will automatically pull on it. I quite often see people walking their dogs down the street with harnesses on and think, "That's one way to ensure the dog does pull." Even dogs on collars and check

collars will pull, because, unlike ours, a dog's neck is full of muscle. The skin is loose and covered by fur. I have seen dogs choking themselves while they pull on the lead, and even this does not stop them pulling.

Dogs also pull because we have not shown them an alternative. Most people, when they lead-train a dog or a puppy, are usually so grateful that they can get them to walk on the lead at all that no attention is given to the finer details of lead training.

A check collar, or choker collar, as it is sometimes wrongly called, is the most effective way to teach a dog to walk on the lead correctly. It is not designed to choke the dog, as many people think, because we know that a dog will choke itself and still pull its owner down the street. The check chain works by sound alone, and also ensures that an over-exuberant dog cannot slip out of its collar. As the dog pulls, the collar tightens; no form of wriggling can get it free, and the collar will loosen again as soon as the dog settles down.

To walk a dog successfully on a check chain, you need to snap the lead back sharply and release it immediately. This makes the metallic sound that the dog will respond to. So when the lead is tight, with the dog straining on it, you should first, very quickly, give some lead—slack is needed to check the dog correctly. Releasing the chain is as important as checking the dog with it. The dog must be made to realize that there is a comfort zone, and if it stays there it will not hear the metallic sound it would prefer not to hear. It is also advisable to use the BAD word at the exact moment the dog is checked, as this will quickly let the dog know that you do not condone the pulling.

Pulling is not the only behavioral problem dogs may display when walking. Many dogs are aggressive toward other dogs that they meet on the walk. Still others are aggressive toward children or adults walking past them.

Traffic orientation is a necessary skill for the modern dog. Some dogs are frightened to death by the loud sounds and great rush of vehicle traffic. Ideally, a puppy should be socialized at an early age to all kinds of strange environments, including the hustle and bustle of traffic. A pup is best able to cope with change at its young age but older dogs can still be trained.

You can use the same method that police use to train their horses. It is a process of desensitization through complete saturation in the environment. Sit at a busy intersection with your dog on a good, secure lead and check chain, reprimanding bad behavior and praising good behavior. Sooner or later the dog will get bored and ignore the passing traffic.

If your dog is one that barks aggressively at traffic you can cure this too. Some dogs require only very aggressive checking of their chain. Others will need the reprimand chain as a diversion. Of course, the dog should be praised the moment it responds.

Most of these problems are based on paranoia, or excessive fear. Sometimes I find that a dog that is displaying aggressive tendencies toward other dogs has a history of an attack on it by another dog, usually when it was a young pup. The bad experience stays with it, and manifests itself as aggression based on fear—the "get-in-first" syndrome. The most effective way to deal with this aggression from a dog toward other dogs or people is to show your dog that you do not condone its antisocial actions. This approach worked with Gengis, the dog in the next case study.

# GENGIS GOES PUBLIC

Gengis was a 12-month-old Rottweiler. He had been a well-adjusted animal up to the age of about five months. Then he was attacked by another dog. This dog's owner finally arrived and beat the dog off both Gengis and his owner. This incident had made Gengis aggressive toward other dogs, and people as well. He was now a highly disturbed dog, with very antisocial behavior.

When I arrived to treat his problem, Gengis tried several times to bite me. The attack had taught him fear of humans and dogs: when the owner of the attacking dog had arrived and begun hitting his dog it would have seemed to Gengis in his terror that both the owner and the dog were attacking him. His only defence from that time on was aggression, the "get-them-before-they-get-me" syndrome.

He seemed to feel he was protecting his owner as well as himself by his aggressive behavior. The attack had been made on both of them, and I was sure he felt his owner condoned his violent actions.

The best way to cure Gengis was to have his owner reprimand him for his actions. Her fear of the attack had probably contributed to his problem, because she would no doubt tighten the lead when other dogs approached, and this would act as a signal to the dog to be aggressive.

I gave her a reprimand chain and instructed her to bring Gengis into the room and throw the chain at the ground near his feet, yelling the BAD word, followed quickly by praise as soon as he reacted. As soon as she led Gengis in, he started barking and growling and lunging at me. She threw the chain and yelled. Gengis immediately responded by sitting down and looking at his owner in disbelief. She patted him lavishly and he immediately began barking and growling at me again. She picked up the chain and repeated the process. He responded in the same way. We continued like this for about fifteen minutes, until he ignored me. I then offered him some doggy treats, and finally had him eating out of my hand. Once he realized that his owner was not happy with his actions he was quite happy to accept me. His owner would now have to repeat the treatment with other people, getting them to do what I had done, and reprimanding him for any aggression.

However, the treatment was far from complete. We still had the aggression toward dogs to address. Starting with a control-led situation would minimize the dangers. We arranged for a friend to walk her dog close to Gengis's fenced yard. We again did the same thing with the reprimand chain as we had done inside the house. It took many reprimands to stop him, but Gengis finally responded to the BAD word alone.

We then faced the biggest challenge of all—going back into the street where the trauma had happened. By now I was able to handle Gengis, so I conditioned him. He was proving to be very responsive, and a highly intelligent animal. In no time he was walking by my side on a loose lead, sit staying and drop staying.

I then took him into the street, accompanied by his owner with the reprimand chain, because he had to concentrate on what he was doing. Every time he stepped forward or pulled on the lead I would snap it. This made him very calm: he had to concentrate on me, and not what was going on around him. He ignored people who walked past, reacted to one barking dog, and finally, after being reprimanded, ignored all other dogs as well. The cure of Gengis was complete.

# Toilet problems

As humans we feel the need to publicly display our possessions by putting our mark on belongings, or by erecting fences on our territory. Dogs are no different except that their ownership is signified by urinating or defecating in strategic areas that will inform intruders that this territory is already claimed. This is called "marking" and is not necessarily restricted by the sex of a dog. Although female dogs usually squat to urinate, some very territorial females will imitate the male and try to cock their legs as high as possible.

Most dogs become quite clean in their toilet habits after an initial settling in period. A pup that was housed inside a concrete pen or kept always inside a house will care little where it goes to the toilet and will not look for grassy areas. If your dog needs toilet training or retraining, never under any circumstances rub its nose in its excretment. To deter a dog from using particular areas as a toilet, place its drinking water in the area. As a rule, dogs will avoid marking near where they eat and drink. Even a dog that is going to be kept inside the house should spend the first few months outside until good toilet habits are re-established, or keep the dog close by and on a lead inside the house so you are aware of its needs. Inside marking can also be discouraged with spraying citronella on the problem areas.

## Chapter Five

# Making Your Dog's Life Easier

# Taking your dog in a car

To a dog, the car is a very strange environment. Not only is the motion of the vehicle unsettling but the space inside the car is compact and enclosed. In such a situation a dog can feel threatened: it feels cornered, as there seems to be no way out. Some dogs may become excited in the car, and bark constantly. Others may run from one side of the car to the other. Remember this when you have your dog in the car for the first time, and ensure that you insist on good manners from the outset. If you let a dog jump or bark, it will think it can always behave this way.

As with most other situations, it is best to get your dog used to the car as early as possible in its life. Try sitting with your dog in the car, just parked in the driveway with the doors open. Try it next time with the doors shut, then with the engine on. After that, attempt a short trip around the block. Soon your dog should understand that it has nothing to fear.

The most effective way to travel with a dog is to tie it with a lead, either to the arm rest or to the seat belt anchor. There are also doggy safety harnesses, which work very well and prevent the dog from jumping all over the car. Once the dog is used to sitting quietly in the car, it can be placed in the car without being restrained.

Squirting a barking dog in a car with water from an atomizer will stop the barking fairly quickly. You can also place a metal receptacle on the floor of the car to amplify sound, and throw the reprimand chain into it when the dog starts barking. This will create a diversion, and if you yell the BAD word also, even the most chronic barkers should abandon this bad habit.

# A visit to the veterinarian or the grooming parlor

As we have seen, dogs learn from experience, and associate bad experiences with the places in which they occur, or the objects or people present at the time of the trauma. It is important that a young dog visits as many new places as possible, especially those that it may have to visit many times.

The veterinarian is one of the most important people in a dog's life. For this reason, animals should never be afraid of visits to or from this person. Take your puppy or new dog along to the veterinarian, just for a first meeting. Have some special treats with you, and get the veterinarian or veterinary nurse offer them to your dog. If you do this regularly, the dog will start to look at the visit to the veterinarian as a pleasurable experience, rather than one that is traumatic.

Another important place to get the dog accustomed to is the grooming parlor. Some dogs are easily frightened, and may suffer traumas here. If possible, take your dog to visit the parlor. Otherwise, visit the grooming parlor alone to assure yourself that the people who run it and work there are the right people to deal with your particular type of dog. If you do take your dog to the parlor for a visit, take doggy treats with you. Make at least four visits with positive results before the dog is first groomed.

The veterinary surgery and the grooming parlor may be environments that bring on other problems such as aggressive behavior between animals when they meet, barking due to fear or nervousness or difficulty in transporting your dog to these places in your car. All these situations are dealt with in separate sections in this book.

# A visit to the kennels

I personally prefer to leave my own dog in his backyard and ask a nearby friend to visit and feed it if I am away for any length of time. I also leave my phone number, and that of my veterinarian. I believe that by not forcing my dog to leave his territory or familiar surroundings, he will suffer less stress.

Nevertheless, there are times when most dogs will have to be boarded at kennels. There is no easy way to introduce your dog to boarding, as any separation from you creates stress. You can help, however, by ensuring that your dog will come to no harm while it is at the kennels.

There are some important points to consider when selecting kennels for your dog. First, you must ensure that the kennels are secure, and your dog cannot escape. Next, you should consider the dog's comfort. The kennels should have a secure exercise area so that your dog can be exercised without escaping, and does not have to remain in a pen for long hours. Also ensure that the owners of the kennels are proficient at handling dogs. If they have bred dogs or handled them for many years they will take good care of your dog. Of course, people who are inexperienced but love dogs may also be suitable, but this fact alone does not make for the efficient control or handling of dogs.

# The aged dog

A dog that is fit and well exercised throughout its life is likely to deal with the aging process far better than less active dogs.

As it ages, your dog requires special consideration. Its diet needs to be altered slightly; for example, it will not be able to digest bones very easily. An aging dog needs less protein than a younger dog, and may need vitamin supplements and appetite stimulants. It may have difficulty absorbing nutrients from its food, and may even have to be given an iron supplement. A veterinarian is the best one to ask about your aging dog's diet. However, there are some dog foods available on the market especially designed for the aging dog.

An aging dog may also have problems with its hearing and its sight. It may get cataracts, and its hearing may begin to fail. Dogs with hearing or visual disabilities can become very bored with life and just mope around. Because of this, we need to make their lives more interesting. We should also assure ourselves that they definitely do have a hearing loss, and not just selective hearing—this can happen with dogs that are that little bit older and more cunning. My 12-year-old dog Gypsy seemed to be going deaf, because when I called her she would just keep on walking and totally ignore my commands. One day I let her out of the house and then called her name. She ignored me, I yelled "Bad!", and she just kept on walking. I then uttered "Dinner," in my normal speaking voice. I have never seen a dog move so fast.

Some dogs do suffer senility as they age but it is more the exception than the rule. It can take many forms: some dogs wander aimlessly, others stand in one spot barking for no readily apparent reason at something unseen. There is no indication that dogs suffer a disease equivalent to Alzheimer's Disease but, like aging humans, they are afflicted with arthritis.

As our aging dogs grow feebler, we may one day have the sad task of deciding whether they should be put to sleep. I had to make that decision about my ever-faithful, beloved Gypsy. She had been a very active dog. We found that not long after her thirteenth birthday she could not walk any more; her spleen had probably ruptured. The veterinarian said he could operate, but there was no guarantee of success, and her age would be against her. With this, and the certainty that her quality of life would be worse if she survived, I had her put to sleep. I remained with her, patting her head, and she went to sleep peacefully. It is important that you stay with your dog at this time so it suffers no stress or anxiety.

A post mortem later showed a huge tumor; Gypsy would not have survived in any case. But even without that new knowledge my decision would have been the same. I believe that when your dog loses its quality of life because of major difficulties such as being unable to walk or constantly bumping into things, it is not living as it would like to. Now the decision must be made, and the owner is the only person who can make this choice. No one else knows your dog better than you do.

A friend once rang me to inform me of the death of his very much loved Dobermann, Pontiac. As our conversation ended, he thanked me for my sympathy. His friends who were not dog lovers could not understand why he was so upset, he said—their comment had been, "It's only a dog."

"Yes," I said. "It's only a dog. Only one of the most faithful and endearing friends you will ever have."

# Index